A CZECH FARM IN MINNESOTA

A CZECH FARM IN MINNESOTA

Janet Holasek Worrall

SPRING CEDARS

Copyright © 2024 by Janet Holasek Worrall

All rights reserved

First edition, 2024

Cover and book design by Spring Cedars
Cover photo: Richard and Evelyn Holasek building
a haystack on their farm in Minnesota, 1950s

ISBN 978-1-963117-23-3 (paperback)
ISBN 978-1-963117-24-0 (hardback)
ISBN 978-1-963117-25-7 (ebook)

Published by Spring Cedars
Denver, Colorado
www.springcedars.com

*In loving memory of
my mother, father, and sister Dorothy*

TABLE OF CONTENTS

FAMILY CHARTS i

PREFACE iii

PART I: BACKGROUND 1

    1. INTRODUCTION 3

    2. HOLASEK FARMS IN MINNESOTA 9

    3. CHASTEK FAMILY IN GLEN LAKE 19

    4. EVELYN SVEC'S LIFE IN HOPKINS 31

PART II: EVELYN HOLASEK'S RECOLLECTIONS 51

    5. FIRST YEARS OF MARRIAGE 53

    6. LIFE IN THE 1930s 67

    7. HIRED HELP 83

    8. BUTCHERING 87

    9. MAKING HAY, HUSKING CORN, THRESHING 93

    10. DAIRY YEARS 105

PART III: JANET HOLASEK WORRALL'S RECOLLECTIONS 119

    11. OBSERVATIONS ON DAILY LIFE 121

    12. VEGETABLE GARDEN 147

    13. DOROTHY AND JANET: GROWING UP 155

    14. DOROTHY AND JANET: SCHOOL DAYS 175

    15. THE SWITCH TO CHICKENS AND BERRIES 187

16. FAMILY AND FRIENDS 207

17. THE HOLASEK HOUSE 231

18. THE HOLASEK BARN 249

19. EPILOGUE 257

ACKNOWLEDGMENTS 289

NOTES.. 293

ABOUT THE AUTHOR... 297

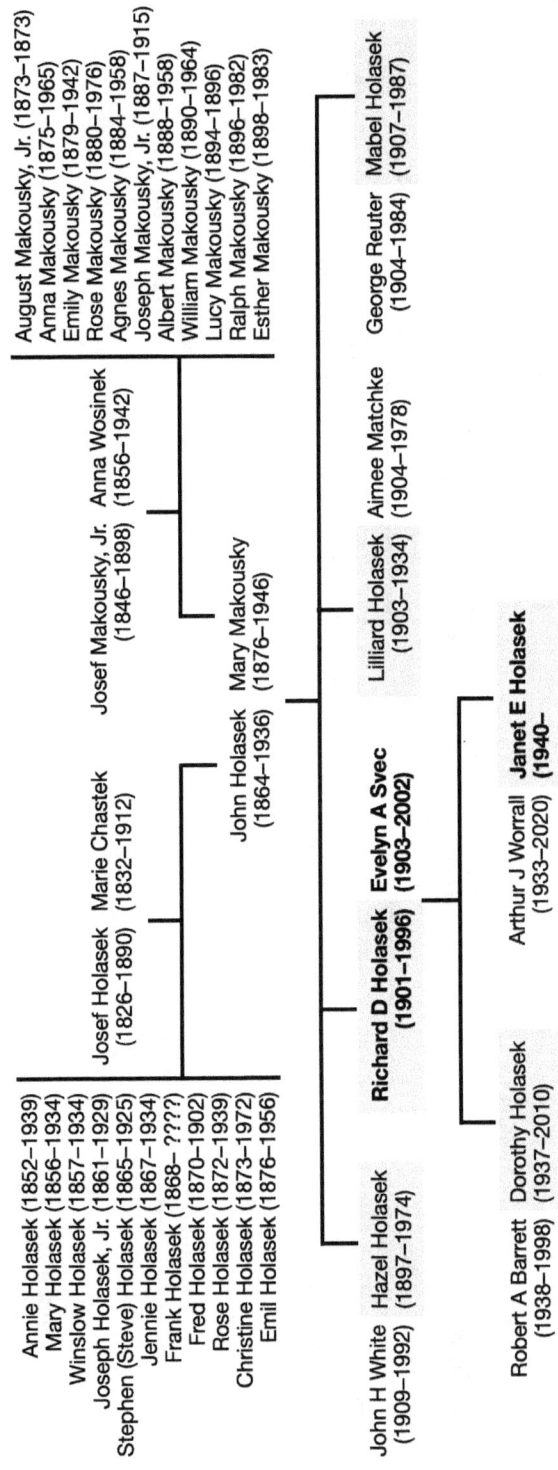

Holasek-Makousky Family Chart

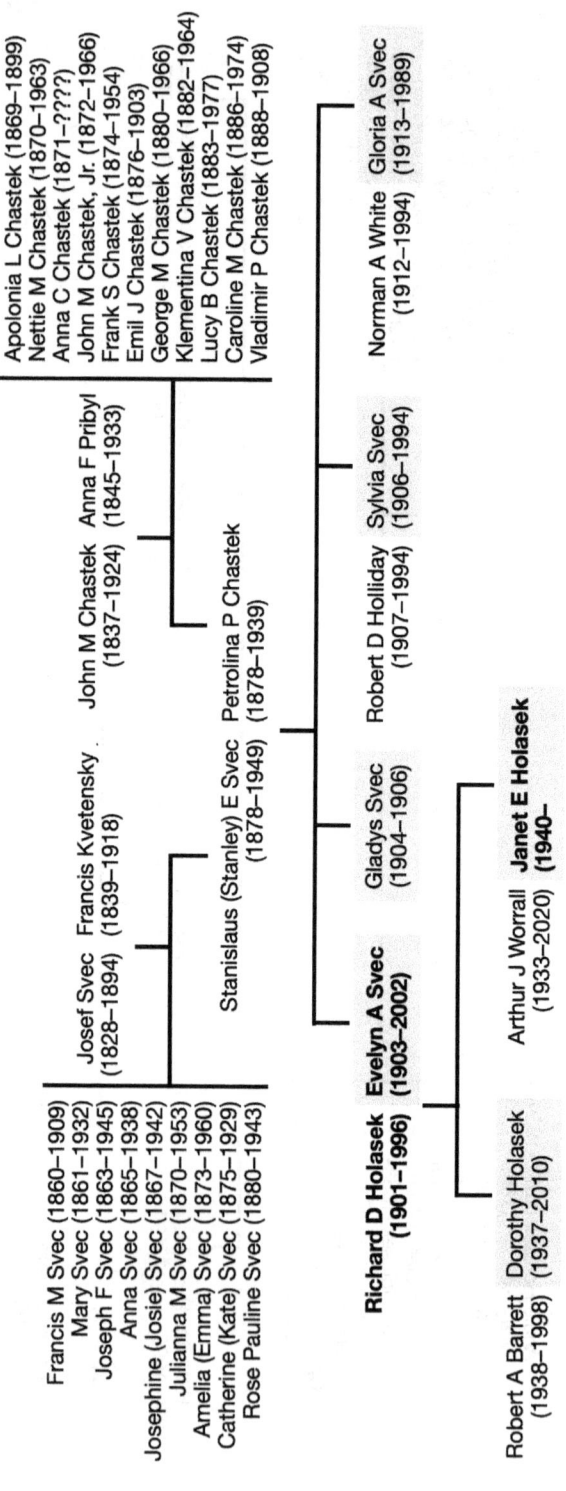

Svec-Chastek Family Chart

PREFACE

This is an account of four Czech families who began their journey from Bohemia to Minnesota in the second half of the 19th century. A central figure is Evelyn (Svec) Holasek who grew up in Hopkins, Minnesota, and was mother to Dorothy and me, Janet. Evelyn married Richard Holasek in 1924, moving from a comfortable town life in Hopkins to a very different life as a farmer's wife in the surrounding rural area.

Evelyn's mother was a descendant of the Částek (later Chastek) family, and her father came from the Swetz (later Svec) family. Evelyn's husband Richard was a descendant of the Holásek (later Holasek) and Makovský (later Makousky) families. These four families all came from Bohemia, which later became part of Czechoslovakia, along with Moravia and Slovakia. Czechoslovakia is now known as the Czech Republic or Czechia and comprises Bohemia and Moravia. Slovakia became an independent country in 1993, officially known as the Slovak Republic. The word "bohemian" has become a popular way to describe a socially unconventional person and in no way should be related or associated with people from Bohemia, part of present-day Czechia.

Part I of this memoir provides a detailed historical background of these families. Parts II and III are personal recollections and stories of daily life from the 1930s into the 1960s. The focus is on the family farm of Evelyn and Richard Holasek in

Eden Prairie, Minnesota, where Dorothy and I grew up. Of particular interest is the role of our mother Evelyn and her life as a farmer's wife, a role that has been given too little attention historically. Also of interest is the evolution of the family farm from the 1920s to its demise, for numerous reasons, by the 1960s.

In part, the purpose of this memoir is to leave a narrative of ordinary lives which often go unnoticed and undocumented but have historical value. I have also written it for my children, grandchildren, and future generations as a record of people and places that have disappeared but are an important part of their heritage. Years ago, my sister Dorothy "Dottie" Barrett and I planned to write this history together. Unfortunately, she left us much too soon in 2010. I will humbly try to represent us both in this account. In growing up, we always referred to our father as Daddy and our mother as Mom, Mommy, or Mother. Later, Mother somehow acquired the nickname Squash, often used fondly by close family members and which she found amusing.

Information for this account comes from many sources. When Mother moved to Fort Collins, Colorado, in 1996, after Daddy died, I taped hours of conversations with her as she reminisced. Her mind and memory never faltered throughout her 99 years. She also left diaries for the years 1931–1937, 1952, and 1958. These often had only one- or two-line entries but provided dates for work in the berries, husking corn, and other chores, which proved to be very helpful. Rather than paraphrasing her, in Chapters 5–10, I decided to use her voice for authenticity. Mother also kept an ongoing family history of facts, photos, and letters from relatives, especially from several aunts on her mother's side. I used these and referenced them in Notes. Occasionally, I added references from newspaper articles and other sources to verify and expand Mother's recollections. I borrowed from *Grandma's Stories* which her grandson Geoffrey Barrett wrote from listening to her reminisce in the 1990s when he visited her in Colorado. I also consulted ship manifests and census records, but anyone using the latter knows they can be inaccurate and inconsistent in content.

As a teenager, I kept diaries for the years 1954, 1955, and 1956, which were useful for recalling events and specific dates. Much later, after Arthur "Art" Worrall and I married in 1967 and moved to Fort Collins, Mother and I kept in touch through letters, which I have used. In these, she kept me up to date on events at home, in Eden Prairie. Finally, my father kept their income tax returns from 1941–1960 that were invaluable in determining annual income, expenses, and dates for farm purchases.

The best source for local events during these years is the *Hennepin County Review,* which is only available on microfilm at the Hopkins Historical Society. During a visit to Hopkins in the fall of 2022, I read several years of this newspaper to fill in details and expand my account. Several monographs, cited in Notes, provided background and context for various subjects.

In writing this book, I have relied on the recollections of many people and make no claim as to their accuracy. Newspaper accounts and census reports may also be inaccurate. But that is the nature of a memoir. It must be viewed within the context of the time and with the acknowledgment that there can be many interpretations of a single event. It is my intent to be as accurate as possible and to have never knowingly written anything that was not true.

PART I:
BACKGROUND

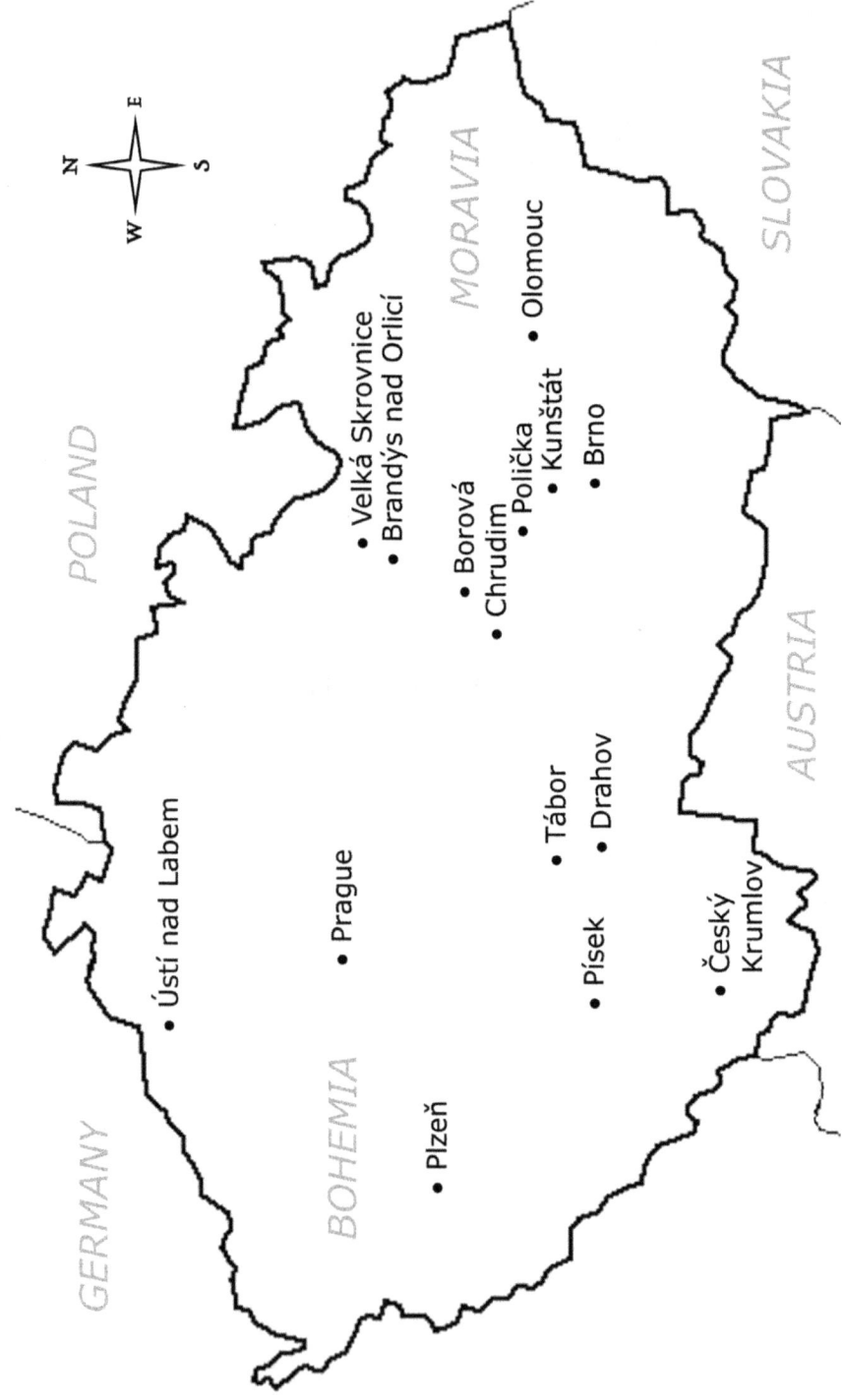

Map of Czech Republic.

1. INTRODUCTION

In the 1850s, the first wave of Czech immigrants left their homeland of Bohemia for America, being attracted particularly to the forested, lake-dotted lands in the Upper Midwest which were opening to settlers. Iowa and Wisconsin had already become states and Minnesota would soon follow in 1858. Handbills circulated throughout Europe advertising the availability of jobs and land. Soon, railroad barons who received thousands of acres of land free from the government would join the efforts to attract people to buy these lands and produce crops using the newly built railroads.

During this migration, the Kingdom of Bohemia (also including Moravia) was part of the Austrian Hapsburg Empire. Peasants labored on the estates of landlords under conditions set forth in the hated *robota*. Briefly stated, this required that peasants provide labor with their draft animals to the lord for three days a week, and six days a week during the harvest season, leaving little time to harvest crops on their own land. Peasants had little incentive to work hard for the lord, and their productivity on his land was estimated at eight to ten times lower than on a peasant's own small piece of land.[1] In addition, while peasant obligations varied, they often included taxes owed to the state, special fees, rent, obligations to the church, and the requirement to use the lord's mill and buy his wine and beer. Giving testimony to this hardship was a Czech emigrant reminiscing:

> We heard that when you worked in America you got money for it. We worked there [Czechoslovakia] in the baron's fields for the scraps left behind. Our tiny piece of land we had bought with many generations of lifetime labor. When the landowner said 'Come to my fields tomorrow,' the men had to go, even though their own crops needed work. If they didn't work fast enough, they were whipped. If they refused to go they were jailed. The baron gave them a few pennies, never more than 20 cents, and many times their own crops spoiled.[2]

The *robota* led to peasant rebellions in 1775, causing the Hapsburg ruler, Empress Maria Theresa, who was also Queen of Bohemia, to bring reform by establishing 11 grades of *robota* labor, each grade with its own requirements. From the peasants' point of view, this did little to improve their situation. Peasant rebellions against the *robota* continued through the 18th and 19th centuries. Finally, in 1848, the *robota* was abolished, but it would be some time before the abolition reached all the distant rural areas. Landlords often ignored the ruling or found ways to circumvent it. Furthermore, peasants with no land still had to work for the lord and submit to his demands.[3]

In addition to the hardship of the *robota*, there were other reasons that led to the decision to emigrate. Military service was compulsory, and families saw their sons conscripted to fight in European wars, often far from home. Natural disasters such as the 1770–1771 floods in Bohemia led to a famine that took half a million lives. Disease threatened in the town of Polička, an area of considerable Czech emigration, with three different outbreaks of cholera in the 19th century. Despite these dangers, the population in the Bohemian crownlands still grew from 4.8 million to 6.7 million between 1815 and 1847. This put enormous strain on families who often had 10 or 12 children and very little land, if any, to distribute. The alternative for many was to leave.[4]

In 1853, two Bohemian immigrants, František Pešek and Joseh Přib, arrived in Minnesota and settled in the wooded, lake area, west of Minneapolis.[5] Finding the location suitable for farming, they wrote to friends back home and urged them to come. The word circulated and, combined with the above reasons, explains why several families—including the Části, Holáseks, Makovskýs, and Brens—decided to leave for America. They all came from what is now the district of Ústí nad Orlicí, a hilly region near the Tichá Orlice and Třebovka Rivers. The town of Ústí had become an important textile center after the 1763 loss of heavily German Silesia to Prussia.[6] But despite this industrial progress, rural areas in the eastern half of Bohemia continued to be controlled by the Czech aristocracy. In 1845, Ústí was connected to the Vienna-Prague railroad via Brno and, in 1850, it was connected to the German border, which gave the Bohemian interior access to German port cities and an avenue for emigrants to leave.

No doubt, considerable interaction existed among the towns in the district of Ústí nad Orlicí, particularly between the towns of Brandýs nad Orlicí and Velká Škrovnice. Families would have known each other for generations, and exchange of produce in town markets and intermarriage would have been common. The district of Ústí nad Orlicí was created in 1960 but, in the 1850s, towns in the district were scattered among the districts of Lanškroun, Vysoké Mýto, and Rychnov nad Kněžnou in the greater area of Chrudim.[7] One group leaving for America included Josef Holásek from Velká Škrovnice and Marie Částek from Brandýs nad Orlicí. They had married on February 23, 1852, in her town. In August 1854, they boarded the train in Ústí for Bremerhaven, Germany, with their one-and-a-half-year-old daughter Annie. Also along were Marie Částek's parents Johann B. Částek and Veronika Suchomel Částek, and their 17-year-old son Jan "John" Částek. Veronika was known as Apolonia by family and affectionately as Babička. On August 13, 1854, they boarded the *Emilie*, beginning a stormy seven-week ocean voyage with nearly everyone getting sick. Upon landing in New York, the Czech passengers took the train to Buffalo, New York. There they caught a ship to cross Lake Erie to Detroit, and then on to Chicago by train, where they rested for two days.

Their next stop was Wisconsin, a state waging an active campaign to attract immigrants from northern and central Europe. Thousands of Germans had settled in the Milwaukee area. Large groups of Protestant Czechs soon joined them, feeling a kinship with the Lutheran Germans and a familiarity with the German language.

The Částek family settled in nearby Racine, Wisconsin, a busy port town on Lake Michigan, with a substantial immigrant population. Needing money for further travel, some of the newly arrived Bohemians found work in nearby Caledonia. There, Johann

Částek and his son John earned money cutting wood, which was in great demand by the railroads. During this time, the Částek family made friends with the Přibyl family, which would have importance later. After a year or two, the Částeks traveled via train to Chicago, and then to Galena, Illinois, where they took a steamboat up the Mississippi River to Fort Snelling. There, they heard about a Bohemian settlement west of Minneapolis. This led them to Minnetonka Township, Minnesota, and the area called Glen Lake where they made their home.[8]

2. HOLASEK FARMS IN MINNESOTA

After landing in New York in 1854 and a brief stay in Racine, Wisconsin, Joseph Holasek (originally Josef Holásek), his wife Marie, and daughter Annie headed for land west of Minneapolis to the adjacent areas of Hopkins, Minnetonka, Glen Lake, and Eden Prairie which attracted newly arriving Bohemians.[9]

Joseph Holasek (1826-1890) and Marie (Chastek) Holasek (1832-1912).

They may have been in contact with an earlier Czech immigrant, František Pešek, who had settled with Joseph Přib on the shores of Shady Oak Lake in 1853. Joseph Přib died shortly after arriving and was buried by the lake. Marie's brother John Chastek (originally Částek) kept in touch with his sister and brother-in-law, which may have drawn the Chastek family to Glen Lake a few years later. František Pešek farmed in the area—John Chastek's memoir mentions Pešek's oxen getting into his father's cornfield and trampling it. In short, the area supported a growing Czech community, which would socialize and lead to intermarriage among the first- and second-generation Czechs.

Joseph Holasek scouted the area for good farmland and built a temporary log cabin on Shady Oak Lake. Over the years, he purchased about 1,200 acres from the government at the going price of $1.15–$1.25 an acre, enough to provide several of his children with farms later. Arriving before the Homestead Act of 1862, immigrants had to purchase land. By the time the Homestead Act went into effect, most of the rich land had been taken, unlike the dryer, treeless prairie lands farther west.

Marie told of an encounter she had with Indians in the area. Once, two came into the cabin, and talking rapidly pointed up and down the stovepipe. But the family couldn't understand what they wanted. As Marie said, the Indians went down to the creek where she kept her axe hidden in the willows—she used the axe to chop ice in the creek and water the livestock. They made off with the axe but were back in a short time to show her a large raccoon they had caught by chopping down a hollow tree.

It would take several years to break the land, plant and produce crops. To survive these first years, Joseph and other men in the area sought work in Minneapolis and St. Paul, especially in the winter when they couldn't work on the farm. In the summer, the rich land and marshes produced wild fruit, cranberries, plums, and grapes. Joseph took advantage of these crops, picking them, even enlisting neighbors to help, and sold them to an eager Minneapolis market. It is reported that one season, he sold 1,600 bushels of cranberries in the Twin Cities. Plums also provided much needed income, and Joseph started his own plum orchard on his land, using the best of the wild plums as seed. He also managed to get some bees which produced honey to replace having to buy scarce and expensive sugar.

Joseph and Marie had 14 children; two died as infants and were buried on a hill nearby with only rough fieldstones for markers. As the number of children grew, the small cabin no longer sufficed. Joseph built a larger log cabin, dismantling the first one and reconstructing it in a more convenient location for use as a chicken house. As the children grew, they helped on the land and also sought work in Minneapolis to supplement the family income. The children in order of their birth were Annie (1852), Mary (1856), Winslow (1857), Joseph Jr. (1861), John (1864), Stephen (1865), Jenny (1867), Frank (1868), Fred (1870), Rose (1872), Christine (1873), and Emil (1876).

The fifth child, John, worked in Minneapolis for several years as a coachman for the Fisk family. In 1896, he married Mary Makousky, from another Czech family living in the area.

Mary Makousky's father was born in Borova, Bohemia, and came to America when he was eight years old. He married Anna Wosinek, born in Racine's Czech community. John Holasek and Mary Makousky had four children: Hazel, Richard (who married Evelyn Svec), Lilliard, and Mabel.

 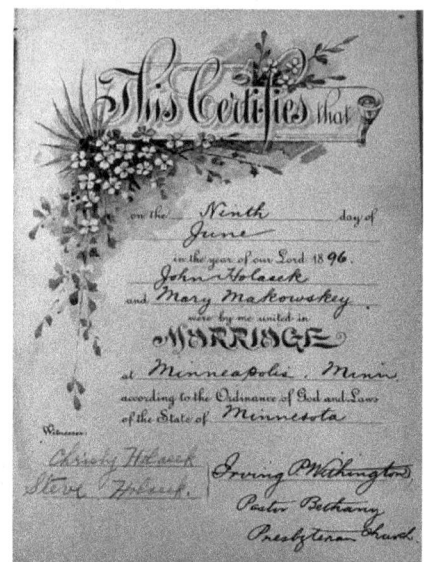

John and Mary (Makousky) Holasek's wedding photo, June 9, 1896, and marriage certificate.

John Holasek's work for the Fisk family probably led to his brother Stephen (known as Steve and Uncle Steve) getting a job as a coachman later for John Pillsbury and his wife Mahala Fisk. John Pillsbury—businessman, philanthropist, and politician—served as Minnesota's governor from 1876 to 1882 and was also a co-founder of the Pillsbury Company. Steve, a very likable and trustworthy person, lived with the Pillsbury family for at least a decade in the early 20th century, working as their coachman. Steve's younger brother Emil hauled hay from the Holasek homestead for Governor Pillsbury's horses. The trip took an entire day. Emil loaded the hay on the wagon the night before and started out early in the morning arriving at the Pillsbury residence in time to have dinner with his brother.

Holasek Farms in Minnesota | 13

Holasek children, left to right: Richard (age 7), Hazel (age 12), Mabel (age 2), Lilliard (age 5).

Steve Holasek standing with horses at Governor Pillsbury's carriage house and stable. Courtesy of Joe Holasek and Laura Helweg.

When John Pillsbury died in 1901, his wife Mahala asked Steve to stay on, which he did until her death in 1910. When not busy with his job, Steve pursued his hobby, working with iron. He made sections of an iron fence and would take them to his farm in Eden Prairie in his free time. Eventually, he built a fence from the main road up to and around the farm buildings and house. He then built square cement posts between sections of fence. Each post was topped with a cement ball about a foot in diameter. In addition, he made several iron settees as outdoor furniture for the farmhouse.

Steve returned to his farm in 1910. Being a bachelor and needing a housekeeper, he hired his cousin Nettie Chastek, a widow. Nettie's husband Casper Videra had died in 1899 after only eight years of marriage, and Nettie had returned to live with her parents John and Anna Chastek. Nettie welcomed the chance to work for

Steve Holasek, c. 1885. Courtesy of Joe Holasek and Laura Helweg.

Fence built by Steve Holasek for the Holasek farm.

Lilliard Holasek going to school in a cutter.

Steve and become independent. Companionship turned to love and, in 1912, Nettie and Steve married. Given that they were cousins and Minnesota forbade the marriage of cousins, the couple had to go to Wisconsin to get married.

Steve's farm was adjacent to his brother John's farm. Steve had watched his nephew Richard grow up and admired him for his work ethic and sense of responsibility. When Steve needed an extra hand to make hay or cultivate corn, he asked Richard to come over. When Steve had a goiter operation and was recovering in the early 1920s, he had Richard live on the farm to take care of the dairy cattle and do other chores. Because Richard was the oldest boy in the family, he had to leave school after eighth grade to help on the farm. His siblings—Hazel, Lilliard, and Mabel—all finished high school.

In the 1920s, the lives of the Holasek and Chastek-Svec families merged, as will be covered in Chapter 4.

3. CHASTEK FAMILY IN GLEN LAKE

Arriving in Glen Lake, around 1856, the Chastek family of three—Johann, Apolonia, and John—settled on government property.[10] What we know of this early settlement comes from the memoir left by the son John. The family's first efforts went toward building a shelter of sod and branches to protect against the weather and intruders. Next, to have food for the coming winter, they planted potatoes and corn. Wild pheasants, ducks, and deer provided meat, and the nearby lakes supplied fish. They purchased 80 acres of land which had to be paid for in the first year at $1.25 an acre. Having no money, they borrowed from the bank at a 36% interest rate. In order to make the payments, John joined his brother-in-law Joseph Holasek in looking for work during the week, likely in Minneapolis. John returned on the weekends to help at home with the farm and his ailing father Johann, who would soon pass away in 1862 at the age of 57. John, now 25, was left in charge of caring for his mother and the family settlement.

The following year, in 1863, John purchased a 160-acre parcel which had seen several owners. In 1857, Robert and Mary Glen had acquired the acreage from the government as a land grant.[11] The Glens sold it to Phebe T. Watson in 1858 for $400. Watson sold the land to Zebulon Ingersoll in 1862. In 1863, Ingersoll sold it to Susan Damon Gale for $700. That same year, it was sold to John for $650.[12]

One reason John's parents left Bohemia was so that he would not be conscripted in the imperial army. Ironically, on August 22, 1864, John volunteered for the Union Army. According to Civil War documents, he enlisted in Company E, Hatch's Independent Battalion of Cavalry. At 27 years old, he was described as 5'7" with brown hair and grey eyes. He served as Reveille at Fort Ripley and, while on duty in June 1865, he suffered an injury to his right side when thrown from his horse. However, he continued to serve until honorably discharged at Fort Snelling on May 1, 1866.

After the war, John returned to manage the family farm in Glen Lake. Deciding it was time to marry, he went to the Bohemian settlement in Racine and wooed 22-year-old Anna Pribyl. He no doubt remembered her family from their earlier contact when he was 17. Anna's parents came from Kunstat, Moravia. Anna's mother Frances Hodr died in 1848 when Anna was three. Her father Ignatz remarried, and the family left Bremerhaven, Germany, arriving in Boston, Massachusetts, on January 5, 1854. The ship manifest lists her father, Francisca (probably Anna's stepmother), four boys (ages 17, 15, 10, and 2), Anna (age 8), and an infant named Joseph. The 1860 census states that Joseph was born at sea. The Pribyl family settled in Racine. When Anna was a young woman, she left Racine and went to Scotland to work as a nursemaid. Unfortunately, there was no information on the circumstances surrounding her time in Scotland but, eventually, she returned to her family in Racine.

After John and Anna married in Racine on March 19, 1868, they headed for Glen Lake. Being a very sociable person, it took

Chastek family, back row left to right: Frank, Nettie, John, Apolonia, Emil; front row left to right: John (father), George, Petrolina, Clementine, Carrie, Lucy, Anna (mother) holding Vladimir. Petrolina made clothes for the whole family without patterns.

Anna some time to settle into the rural Glen Lake area. But once they started a family, Anna kept busy with her children as well as helping on the farm. Life was not easy. Anna had to go to a nearby lake to get water to wash clothes and then had to heat the water on a wood stove. Anna gave birth to 11 children between 1869 and 1888. Her mother-in-law Apolonia lived with them and helped with household tasks and the children until her death in 1885.

John was an ambitious and energetic man. He grew wheat and an abundance of fruit trees and raspberries for income. The dairy cattle provided milk and cream; Anna skimmed off the cream to make butter, which John took to his customers in Minneapolis every two weeks. Any milk not consumed by the family was fed to the hogs that they raised as another source of income. The dressed hogs sold for $0.03 a pound.[13]

On January 11, 1890, at age 53, John applied for an invalid pension due to his Civil War injury. It is unclear why he waited so long, but he declared that he was greatly disabled and that his work as a farmer required manual labor, a difficult task due to his disability from the war injury.[14] In support of John's application, Winslow Naly, who had served with John, gave the following testimony.

> I being of Co. E Independent Battalion Minn Cav. know John Castek of same company that on or about May 1865 at Fort Ripley, Minnesota. I saw him while mounting he was thrown from his horse. When he was lifted up he was unable to speak. He was placed in wagon and taken along with… He could not ride in saddle for few days and since then he often complain of dull pain in his head and right-side caused from the injury he received at Fort Ripley…I did not see comrade Castek for about two months. When Co. got together again he did not look well and did not seem to improve during the time I last saw him.[15]

Eventually, John received a pension of $75 a month until his death in 1924. Anna then received $50 a month until her death in 1933.

By the early 1900s, the Chasteks looked toward selling some of their land as well as passing pieces along to their children. Fortuitously, in 1907, the Minnesota Legislature approved funding for a detention home for boys ages 13–20 in a "cottage system" farm home. It was designed for young boys whose delinquency did not merit their being sent to the reform school in Red Wing, Minnesota, but who needed more help than just being put on probation. With educational and vocational guidance in the right setting, they could become responsible citizens. In 1908, the Hennepin County Commissioners bought 92 acres (the total for the school would eventually be 167 acres) from John and other farmers for $11,000. The purchase included the Chastek's 10-room farmhouse, barn, chicken coop, and outbuildings. The institution was officially known as the Hennepin County Juvenile Detention Home, but locals knew it as the Glen Lake Farm School for Boys. The boys arrived in 1909, with a total of 54 in the first year. The school publicized its goal as offering the revolutionary idea of reforming young boys rather than incarcerating them. Their offenses included burglary, disorderly conduct, jumping onto moving trains, general delinquency, incorrigibility, and driving away a horse without the owner's consent.

Over the years, the number of buildings increased, a Girls' School Program was added, and there were changes with less emphasis on the farm aspect of training. As time passed in the 21st century, the emphasis on community-based treatment methods grew, and the number of youths at the farm school declined. This plus the need to modernize the aging facility led to its closure in 2021, after having been in operation for over a century. Testimonials by some of the boys show that for many, the school had achieved its goal of shaping responsible adults.[16]

A few years after John sold land for the Glen Lake Farm School for Boys, he sold all but 12 acres of his remaining property to Hennepin County and, later, to the state of Minnesota for a tuberculosis sanatorium. One can get an idea of the lay of the land and why John's parents chose to settle in Glen Lake from a description that the sanatorium commission used in making the selection of the site.

> The area, known as Little Switzerland, provided an expansive view of hills, marshes, and woods. It fulfilled the recommendations that the sanatorium be placed...on the southern exposure of a hill in an area of natural beauty to help 'amuse patients and keep them contented.'[17]

Tuberculosis had become a growing threat to the nation's health with no cure in sight except to alleviate symptoms with rest, fresh air, and nutritious food. In the late 19th and early 20th centuries, the sanatorium concept of isolating tuberculosis patients became the prevailing treatment. The openness and fresh air of northern Minnesota attracted attention and, in 1907, a sanatorium opened near Walker. This was followed by other efforts to isolate and treat children and adults in camps and sanatoriums. But Minnesota lacked a large facility near the population center of Minneapolis with transportation to enable families to visit patients.

In 1913, the state legislature appropriated $500,000 for counties to use as matching funds for the building of sanatoriums. Construction began on the Glen Lake Sanatorium the following year with equal contributions from both the state and county. At its opening in January 1916, the sanatorium provided three cottages with a total of 50 beds for patients. According to records, the first patient arrived on a sleigh in a raging snowstorm! In the 1920s, major remodeling and expansion took place as it became the largest sanatorium in Minnesota. A streetcar ran from Glen Lake to Minneapolis, but reaching the sanatorium required a three-quarter-mile walk from the end of the streetcar line. To alleviate the problem, the sanatorium provided transportation with a horse and wagon. Eventually, buses from Minneapolis came regularly to the sanatorium and provided transportation not only for those associated with it but also for the surrounding population.

At the height of its operation, 718 patients were being treated. In the 1950s and particularly in the 1960s, the number of patients declined with the use of antibiotics to treat tuberculosis. The Oak Terrace Nursing Home operated in the sanatorium from the 1960s through the 1980s. A paper transfer was made for the last tuberculosis patient from the sanatorium to the nursing home in 1976.[18] For over half a century, the Glen Lake Sanatorium was a landmark with its U-shaped construction. In 1993, the building was demolished, representing the conquering of a disease that had taken thousands if not millions of lives. A golf course now rests on the site.

Over the course of many years, John and Anna Chastek gave each of their sons land to farm. The amount varied from 10 to 60 acres depending on the location and usage. The daughters received $250 when they married.[19] On the land that they still owned, John and Anna built themselves a new home with all the modern

Glen Lake Sanatorium.

Chastek family home in Glen Lake, built c. 1910.

conveniences: a tiled bathroom, furnace and, later, electricity and a telephone. Relatives who visited praised the spacious rooms, indoor toilet, and modern design. Their son George built a house for his family on an adjacent acre. John and Anna continued to live on their land in Glen Lake where they celebrated their 50th wedding anniversary on March 19, 1918.[20]

Their son Frank received 10 acres nearby on which he had an apple orchard and raised mainly raspberries along with some

John and Anna Chastek's 50th wedding anniversary, 1918.

strawberries, gooseberries, and currants. Frank married Marenka "Marie" Sykora and one of their children, Vivian (1909–1999), left a wonderful account of her childhood.[21] She walked about two miles to elementary school. To get to the high school in Hopkins, she took the streetcar which also went to Minneapolis, where her mother would go to shop in the department stores. Her brother Enrico trapped muskrats and sold the skins. He also sold newspapers at the newly built sanatorium, and Vivian would occasionally go with him. They were hesitant to enter the front office for fear of getting tuberculosis, but the nurses assured them they would be in no danger. In the summer, they fished in the nearby lakes and in the winter, went ice-fishing. Fish were plentiful, and there was no stocking of the lakes.

In the summer, Vivian picked berries and often went with her dad to Minneapolis where he sold them at the farmers market. They had a Baby Grand Chevrolet, and she and her brother and cousins took turns going to market. A special treat was having breakfast at the market restaurant, as people rarely ate out in those days. Occasionally, they went to the movies, and Vivian remembers the first one she saw in the Hopkins theatre, *Birth of a Nation*.

Vivian gives one of the few references found to the 1918–1919 influenza epidemic. When she was about ten, she remembers Aunt Nettie and Uncle Steve coming in their one-horse sleigh to bring Christmas presents. They wore gauze masks, did not come inside the house, and left the gifts by the door. Vivian doesn't remember anyone who had the flu but knew everyone feared contracting it and took precautions to stay safe. This would have been December of 1918, following serious outbreaks in the fall of 1918.

According to Curt Brown's book, *Minnesota, 1918*, beginning October 13, 1918, Minneapolis banned all public gatherings. On November 1, the *St. Cloud Daily Times* reported 72 deaths from the flu in the previous ten days. Newspapers tended to downplay the epidemic and, in October, said it was under control, but October would be the worst month for deaths. Hospitals experienced a shortage of doctors and nurses to treat the sick due to medical personnel serving in Europe during the war. While Minnesotans never experienced the huge loss of life other states endured, the flu took the lives of 12,000 people in the state.[22]

Vivian's years in Minnesota were numbered. In 1919 or 1920, her father saw a motion picture advertising land in California. Curious, he went to explore and bought 20 acres in Brentwood. He and his son Enrico built a small cottage on the land and, in November 1920, the family moved to California.

The Chastek family was known to take care of the next of kin, especially when tragedy struck. Apolonia, John and Anna's first child—named after her grandmother—was born in 1869. She married Edward Bren, and they had two children, Clementine and Adelaide. In 1899, when Apolonia was only 30 years old, she died giving birth to their third child, Apolonia. Edward and the Bren family raised the oldest girls while grandmother Anna and her daughter Nettie helped raise Apolonia. The census for 1900 lists

Nettie as 29 and Apolonia G. Bren as 2 years old, both living in the Chastek-Pribyl household. Apolonia continued to live with them until her marriage to Vladimir A. Nayek on June 27, 1916.

John Chastek passed away from a stroke in May 1924 at the age of 87. Anna rented the house in Glen Lake to a doctor at the sanatorium and moved to Hopkins to live with her daughter Nettie. Anna lived almost another decade before she died tragically in an automobile accident in September 1933 at the age of 88. She and daughters Nettie and Clementine were going to Pierz, Minnesota, to visit a third daughter, Carrie. Nettie was driving when the car overturned, apparently due to a faulty steering apparatus. Anna was killed instantly; Nettie and Clementine suffered injuries but did not require hospitalization. A sad ending for Anna who lived a long and memorable life.[23]

This narrative continues with John and Anna Chastek's sixth child Petrolina (1878–1939) who went by the nickname Pet. She married Stanley Svec from Hopkins in 1902. They had four daughters; the oldest was Evelyn. She married Richard Holasek in 1924 and is a central figure in this story.

4. EVELYN SVEC'S LIFE IN HOPKINS

In 1879, the Joseph Swetz (later Svec) family left St. Catherine, Co. of Chrudim, Bohemia, for the northern German port of Bremerhaven to board the *SS Leipzig* destined for Baltimore, Maryland. The family consisted of Joseph, a tailor and shoemaker, his wife Francis Kvetensky, a midwife and pregnant at the time, and nine children ranging from 19-year-old Francis Marie, to 18-month-old Stanislaus. Stories passed down through generations allege that Stanislaus learned how to walk on board the ship but, given his age, probably walked before boarding the *SS Leipzig*. Upon landing in Baltimore, they headed for Racine, again where many Bohemians settled before moving to the interior. The family stayed there a few months then went to Milwaukee where Francis gave birth to Rose Pauline on January 25, 1880. They probably stayed in Milwaukee until 1885 when Joseph, Francis, and the younger children moved to St. Paul, Minnesota, with its growing Czech community. At some point, Francis's brother Frank Kvetensky (1842–1898) joined them.

When Joseph died in 1894, the three youngest children, Rose Pauline, Stanislaus "Stanley," and Catherine "Katie" lived with their mother in St. Paul. While in St. Paul, 17-year-old Rose Pauline had a brief marriage to Thomas F. Lenc in May 1897, bearing a child, Alice Rose (1897–1967). They divorced on November 16, 1899.

Young Stanley Svec.

Joseph Svec's application for citizenship, 1884 (family in Wisconsin) (left). Declaration of Joseph Svec's citizenship, 1888 (family had moved to Minnesota) (right).

Svec family trunk probably brought to America from Bohemia.

Dishes brought by Svec family from Bohemia.

Joseph and Francis (Kvetensky) Svec with their two youngest children, Stanley and Rose Pauline, 1890.

Immigrating to Minnesota around the same time as the Svec family was the Koblas family, also coming from Bohemia from the town of Drahov, south of Prague.[24] The father Frank Koblas died in Bohemia in 1876. After his death, his widow Katerina Vechra Koblas and children (four sons and two daughters) left for the United States. Whether they came as a group or individually is unknown. Catherine "Katie" married in Eau Claire, Wisconsin, in 1880. Several others settled in New Prague, Minnesota, joining its large Czech community, where the oldest son James F. Koblas (1856–1937) married Catherine Zita in 1883. A few years later, the couple moved to Hopkins where James opened a butcher shop on the town's main street, which became Excelsior Avenue. Seeing possibilities for the growing town, James built a large commercial building known as the Koblas Block on Excelsior Avenue. He moved his meat market to the ground floor of the new structure in 1892 and soon added a grocery business.[25]

The Svec and Koblas families joined in both marriage and business. Rose Pauline Svec married James's younger brother John James Koblas (1870–1918) on December 20, 1899, in Hopkins. John worked in the grocery business with James. Shortly after the marriage, John and Rose Pauline went to Bristol, South Dakota, to open a meat market but returned to Hopkins in 1901 to run a grocery store with Stanley Svec. After two years, John and Rose Pauline went back to South Dakota and opened a store in Utica. Stanley Svec then had his own grocery store on the ground floor of the Independent Order of Odd Fellows (IOOF) building which was across the street from the Koblas Block. Stanley's store had the advantage of being on the corner of 9th and Excelsior Avenue where the streetcar ran.[26]

In 1900, Hopkins (also known as West Minneapolis) thrived as a commercial center for the surrounding agricultural areas, many settled by Bohemians. A main employer, the Minneapolis Threshing Machine Company (MTM), moved to Hopkins in 1887. Its employees lived in the nearby tenement known as the Beehive, the Hollister Hotel, and West Minneapolis House. After weathering the 1893 Depression, the factory attracted another wave of Bohemian immigrants, requiring that more housing be built. Three railroads ran through the Hopkins area: James J. Hill's Great Northern (now the BNSF), Minneapolis and St. Louis (M&StL), and Milwaukee Road. In the 1890s, Thomas B. Walker built an electric streetcar line from Minneapolis to St. Louis Park which reached Hopkins by 1897.[27] Streetcars gave residents access to Minneapolis and St. Paul. Grocery stores, barber shops, public baths, saloons, livery stables, meat markets, and lodges dotted the main street of Hopkins, satisfying peoples' daily needs. By 1906, the population reached 1,648.

Czechs were very sociable people and, as a place for them to meet, Frank and Annie (Holasek) Kinsel donated land for a ZCBJ Lodge (Western Bohemian Fraternal Association), library, and meeting hall in Glen Lake. In 1871, Annie Holasek married Frank Kinsel who left Bohemia for the United States in 1861. Early Czech families helped build the hall in the 1880s and, for over half a century, it became the center for dances, Sokol gatherings, parties, picnics, and scheduled lodge meetings. Unfortunately, due to a furnace malfunction or carelessly tossed cigarette, it caught fire and burned after a New Year's

Stanley Svec (wearing apron) in his grocery store on Excelsior Avenue, one clerk behind counter, two clerks (sisters) standing by Stanley, c. 1914.

County Fair in Hopkins, c. 1906.

Eve banquet in January 1933. For years, it had been the gathering place where Czechs met friends and potential marriage partners.[28]

Sokol was one of the most popular activities among the Czechs. It began in Bohemia in the 1860s and rapidly transferred to America with immigrants. Emphasizing pride in nationality and unity, Sokol promoted athleticism, believing that one had to be physically fit to be mentally and emotionally healthy. Entire families competed in gymnastic activities. Men used bars and rings while women did exercises. Children participated in their own age groups. Competitions were held between surrounding towns with large Czech populations like Montgomery, Jordan, Owatonna, and New Prague. Indicative of its importance, three women represented Hopkins at the 1925 National Sokol Gymnastic exhibition in Chicago.[29]

The large Czech populations in Hopkins and adjacent Glen Lake came together for dances in Bohemian venues and gatherings of

ZCBJ pin.

Sokol. At some point, Stanley Svec became acquainted with and began to woo Petrolina Chastek, the lovely daughter of John and Anna Chastek. With her black hair and sparkling blue eyes, Petrolina was a stunning young woman. On June 18, 1902, they married in Glen Lake and moved to Hopkins near Stanley's grocery store. The following year, they had their first child Evelyn. A few years later, Gladys was born.

Stanley and Petrolina (Chastek) Svec's wedding photo, June 18, 1902.

Sisters Evelyn and Gladys Svec, c. 1907

Stanley and Petrolina Svec's house at 105 9th Avenue North, Hopkins, where Evelyn Svec grew up, built in 1902, photo taken c. 2010.

Gladys lived less than two years, and one of Evelyn's first memories was watching her mother's tears flow as she sewed Gladys's burial dress. Stories indicate that Gladys died from eating poisonous berries, but that is questionable since she died in January. Perhaps she died of food poisoning or an intestinal ailment. Two more daughters were born: Sylvia in 1906 and Gloria in 1913.

Evelyn—a feisty, energetic, creative woman, loved by everyone who met her—is a central figure in this narrative. She outlived all her siblings, living her first 93 years in the Hopkins-Eden Prairie area and her last six in Colorado, missing her 100th birthday by eight months. But that is getting ahead of our story.

Evelyn began working in her father's grocery store when she was seven or eight years old. She stocked shelves and particularly liked handling the fragrant Rose Cream Soap, a laundry soap. Women would slice the soap into a big boiler of water, add the clothes, and let them boil to sterilize and clean them. As Evelyn grew older, she advanced to being a clerk, scooping flour, sugar, and rice from open bins, switching languages from English to Czech, depending on the customer.

Evelyn's work in the store did not take her away from school, as education had a high priority among Bohemians. Because they often lived and worked together, children, parents, and grandparents spoke only the Czech language. Evelyn entered first grade knowing no English and had to learn it by immersion as did many others. Learning English never seemed to be a barrier or caused her any trauma as a child, probably because it was the natural thing to do. She did remember that she and her sisters had only one school dress which they wore all week. It would be washed on the weekend so it was fresh for the next week. When Evelyn entered seventh grade, she had her first store-bought dress. It was velvety and heavy, but she really didn't like it, even though everyone said it was pretty!

Stanley's mother Francis Svec left St. Paul to live with Stanley when he moved to Hopkins. Her husband Joseph had died in 1894. Francis had studied medicine in Bohemia and had to send for her diploma before she could practice. Her services as a midwife were much in demand. When news of an impending birth arrived, Stanley would hitch up the horse and buggy in the summer, or sleigh in the winter, and take her to her patient. Francis would stay there for a few days to care for the mother and newborn before Stanley would come to bring her back home. There she had her own room with a

Joseph and Francis Svec's headstone in Calvary Cemetery, St. Paul, Minnesota.

stove to brew herbal medicines for which she earned considerable fame. When Evelyn contracted diphtheria, a dreaded disease at that time and long before there was a vaccine, Grandma Svec stayed with her night and day to make sure her breathing passages stayed open, no doubt saving her life.

Joining other Czechs, the entire Svec family competed in Sokol events. Photos of the Hopkins Sokol show Petrolina and Stanley in the Sokol uniform. Stanley was muscular and powerful, and Evelyn told of watching him walk up and down the steps on his hands. The leaders gave awards for excelling in groups. Evelyn wore her Sokol Eagle award on a chain well into her nineties. It was one of her proudest possessions.

Evelyn Svec's Sokol Eagle award.

Petrolina Svec (bottom left), Sokol, c. 1915.

Stanley Svec (bottom left), Sokol, c.1915.

Evelyn spent summers with her best friend Anna Tiro. The two roller-skated all over Hopkins, picked wild strawberries along the railroad track, and walked two miles to go swimming or ice-skating in the winter. In the evenings, a group would gather to play pom-pom-pullaway, hide-and-seek, kick the can, and other games, or just to have races in the street.

Sometimes, fun turned tragic as happened when Evelyn's sister Sylvia was playfully pushed by a friend into a newly dug cellarway. Sylvia landed on a rusty nail that penetrated her foot so deeply that her dad had to use pliers to pull it out before rushing her to the doctor. The swelling got worse as blood poisoning set in. There was little to be done, and it appeared she would lose her leg if not her life. Everyone was devastated. A man nearby heard of the accident, came and talked to Stanley, and the two of them went to a neighbor's farm to get fresh cow manure. Petrolina put the manure around Sylvia's foot, wrapped it, and waited. By morning, the swelling had gone down, and gradually the wound healed. Sylvia never forgot the man's lifesaving gesture and, years after he had died, she regularly went to the cemetery to put flowers on his grave.[30]

Evelyn also had a close call but of a different sort. Her dad liked to hunt with his friends. Several photos exist of Stanley and his friends hanging out or standing by deer they had shot. After one of these outings, Stanley came into the kitchen with his hunting rifle, not knowing that it was loaded. He propped it in the corner of the kitchen, and it suddenly fired, narrowly missing Evelyn. Stanley's face turned ashen. He took the rifle out of the house, and it was never seen again.

Stanley (second from the left) with his hunting friends.

As Evelyn got older, her responsibilities in the family grocery store grew. When her dad left on errands, she had charge of the store. As winter approached in 1918, Stanley decided to go to his brother-in-law Steve Holasek to cut wood—then the source of heat along with coal. While climbing a tree, Stanley slipped and fell, badly hurting his back. It took him several weeks to recover, and he stayed on the farm with Steve and his wife Nettie (Petrolina's sister). Evelyn, only 15 years old, had to open and close the store and secure the money in the safe. It happened to be Armistice Day, celebrating the end of the Great War. The clerks came to Evelyn saying that all the other stores had closed and they wanted to join the crowds in the street. But there was one delivery yet to be made, and it fell to Evelyn. So she and her cousin got into Stanley's old truck, which had to be cranked to start, and off they went. Evelyn made the delivery but left the truck running so she wouldn't have to crank it again. Sure enough, when she got back to the truck, the engine had stopped and she had to crank it again—no easy task for a 15 year old!

The janitor in the grocery store, Roy Marsh, boarded with the Svecs. He had no family and, when he could no longer work, moved to what was known in Hopkins as the Poor Farm, built in 1865 and rebuilt in 1878 after a fire destroyed the first building. There, men without families or with disabilities, worked as much as possible on the farmland and were well cared for. Every year on Roy's birthday, Petrolina would take the streetcar and walk the extra mile to see him. She brought him some tobacco, knowing he liked to smoke. She did that for many years until one year when she went, she was told he had died. No one had let her know that he was ill, and she was devastated that he had probably died alone.

Evelyn graduated from Hopkins High School June 6, 1921, at 8:00 p.m. in the Opera Hall, a building on the Koblas Block. She along with 20 other students received their diplomas from W.S. Smetana. The class flower was a tea rose, and the class motto was "On." This captured the optimism and energy of the young graduates as they faced the decade of the 1920s.

Evelyn then took a secretarial course at the Minneapolis Business College, finishing on August 6, 1921. She accepted a position with a Hopkins attorney and was particularly helpful with older clients who spoke only Czech, as Evelyn remained fluent in Czech and English.

With the appearance of the automobile, mobility increased for young people. They went to dances, visited friends, gathered to listen to primitive radios, and began to pair off with serious partners.

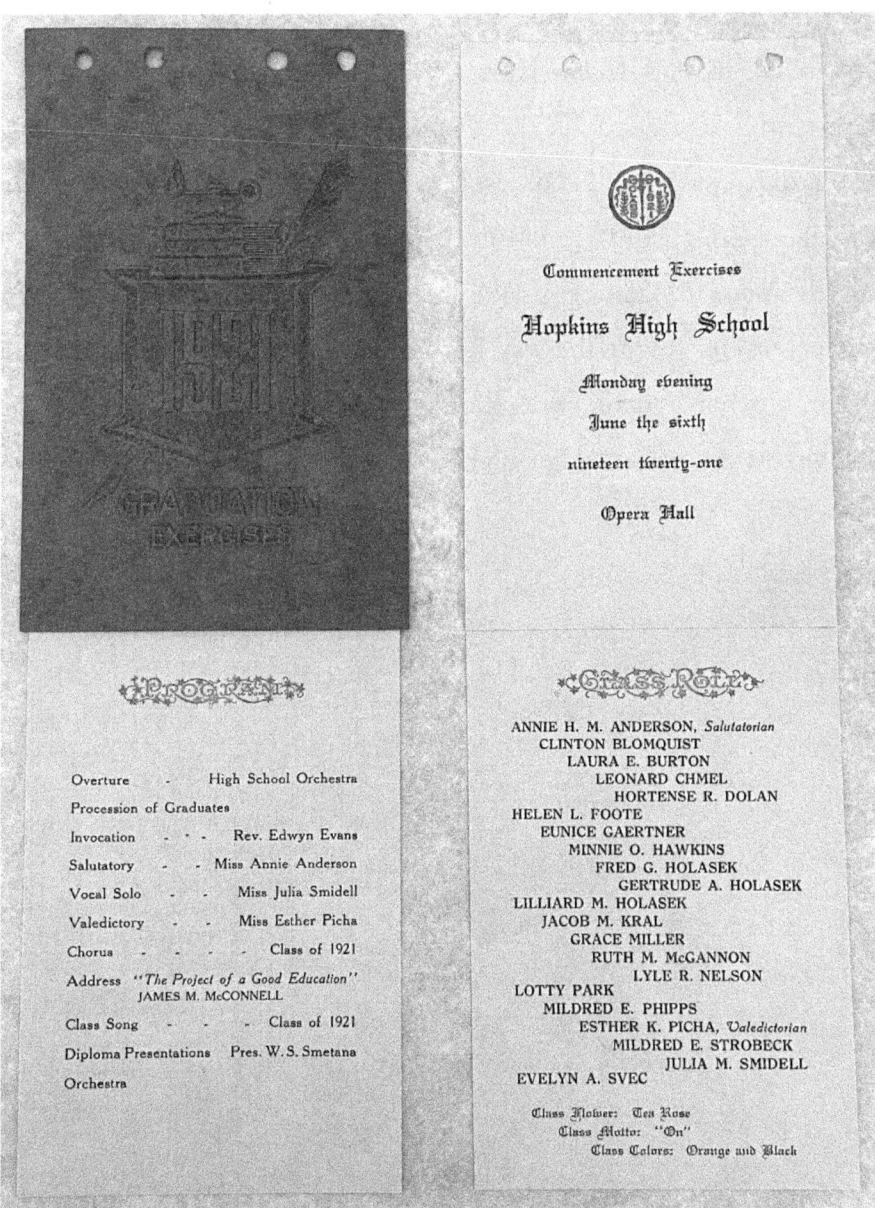

Evelyn Svec's 1921 high school graduation program.

The Chastek, Svec, and Holasek children went to the same school, had common Czech roots, and lived in the same locale. So, not surprisingly, Evelyn started dating her classmate Lilliard Holasek, son of John and Mary Holasek. But Lilliard saw an attraction between Evelyn and his brother Richard. Two years older than Lilliard, Richard was the oldest boy in the family. He had to drop out of school after eighth grade to help on the farm and thus was at a disadvantage in getting to know young people. Lilliard gallantly stepped aside, paving the way for his brother Richard to date Evelyn. Later, Evelyn allowed that Richard was more fun! Little did she know how dramatically her life would soon change.

PART II:
EVELYN HOLASEK'S RECOLLECTIONS

5. FIRST YEARS OF MARRIAGE

Fortunately, Uncle Steve and Aunt Nettie decided to retire in 1924. Knowing of Richard "Dick" and my plans to marry, Uncle Steve decided to sell his 85-acre farm to Dick. I put all the money I had saved toward the purchase. We agreed to pay $9,000 and to pay the survivor, Steve or Nettie, $350 annually for the rest of his or her life. Payment was to be made by December 3rd of each year. Uncle Steve promised to lease us the machinery and cattle on the farm as part of the bargain. The verbal agreement concluded with a handshake.

Richard and Evelyn (Svec) Holasek's marriage certificate.

Richard and Evelyn (Svec) Holasek's wedding photo, with attendants Sylvia Svec (Evelyn's sister) and Lilliard Holasek (Richard's brother) standing, December 12, 1924.

We married on December 12, 1924, and tragedy struck the first year of our marriage. Uncle Steve's goiter surgery seemed to have affected his mind, as after the surgery his behavior changed. He'd go into the basement and stay there a very long time for no reason. One day, he climbed to the top of the high windmill and walked around the top. There was no reason for this, but now I think he was contemplating suicide. On Monday, June 1, 1925, Dick and I were laying linoleum in the dining room while Aunt Nettie worked in the next room, cleaning. Dick's father John came in and asked, "Where is Steve?" We thought he was in the barn. John whispered something to Dick, and the two left. They came back to tell us that Steve had committed suicide by shooting himself. On hearing it, Aunt Nettie screamed and screamed so loudly that I had to go into the basement to escape her shrieking.

The police came and accused Dick of killing Steve. They put Dick in the back seat of the police car making him sit next to the pile of Steve's bloody clothes. The police questioned me, and I said, "yes," I had heard a shot while Dick and I were laying linoleum, but thought nothing of it as many people came around to hunt squirrels, and hearing a shot was not uncommon. In those days, a wife's testimony meant nothing, so the police drove off with Dick. They stopped at a restaurant for lunch, leaving Dick alone in the car, perhaps thinking that if he were guilty, he'd use the chance to escape. Finding him still in the car when they returned from lunch, the police eventually brought him home in the evening. Meantime, I had to go down to milk the cows. Thank goodness Dick's father came over, pulled up a stool, and helped me. A day or two later, Dick was summoned to the county morgue to give evidence in the death of Steve Holasek.

To add to the trouble, I remember a terrible storm came through the next day. A tornado tore through Eden Prairie, Hopkins, and then St. Louis Park, causing millions of dollars in damage and killing seven people. It picked up a 500-foot-long Moline warehouse and smashed it into the old streetcar bridge in addition to destroying other buildings. It tore off the roof and crushed part of the Minneapolis Threshing Machine (MTM) building. I was home alone and terrified. The house just shook.[31]

Now a widow, Nettie reneged on the verbal agreement between Dick and Steve to lease us the machinery and cattle. She auctioned off everything, leaving Dick and me without any income. This led to bitterness, especially between Dick and Nettie. Dick blamed my family, particularly my mother Petrolina Chastek, and thought she could dissuade Nettie from the sale, but Nettie felt she needed the money, having no source of income after Steve's death. She went to live with her parents in Glen Lake again, having lost her second husband.

Our local paper, *The Hennepin County Review*, had a front-page story reporting Steve's death and indicated that his suicide was because he was despondent over the sale of his farm and wanted to buy it back but couldn't.[32] I do not know where this information came from, but it is highly unlikely as Steve liked Dick and was happy with our marriage. I still believe that his suicide was caused by his goiter surgery, as surgery had side effects that we do not have today.

This issue with Nettie remained a constant irritant for the rest of our marriage, as she continued to want more than $350 annually. Eventually, the payments increased to $500. In 1960, when the state took 26 acres of our farm for Interstate 494, Nettie wanted a share of the $53,000 settlement. Her attorney got her $12,800, but Nettie was not satisfied. She was bothered that her nephew still had two-thirds of the land to sell, and she wanted a share of that. Her attorney suggested that we give her $2,500 more with the understanding that it would end any future claim she had to the land and would also end her annual payments. We agreed. At the time, she was 90 years old. She died three years later, in 1963.

After the sale of the machinery and cattle, survival for us depended on the 40 acres of raspberries that Dick and Lilliard had planted. The patch was enormous with 49 rows of 171 bushes per row. Many farmers in the Hopkins area made their livelihood from growing raspberries and strawberries. Hopkins was known as the raspberry capital of Minnesota.

In late June 1925, the first raspberry pickers came. It was quite an adjustment for me after leading a stenographer's life in town! Berry season began in late June and lasted until the end of July. We boarded berry pickers for about ten years, usually about 20 young women, depending on the year's crop. I remember because I'd bake three pies, cut each into seven pieces and have one piece left for Dick. We never had to advertise for pickers but usually got

Evelyn Holasek standing in neighbor's strawberry patch, c. 1925.

names from Dick's folks or neighbors who all had to hire pickers. They usually came from Czech areas around Montgomery, Minnesota, and were young women and a few older ladies, no men. We tried a few boys, but they did not have the ambition the women had. We did not have them return while many of the young women returned year after year. They boarded in the house for the season of four to six weeks. Each bedroom had two beds, and the larger room above the kitchen had three beds, while a few slept on the front porch. That involved a lot of bedding, which took work to get ready and launder during berry season.

For a few years, Dick took the crated berries to the farmers market in Minneapolis in our Ford pickup truck. In 1929, he started taking them to the Excelsior Fruit Growers Association which meant a much shorter trip as well as shorter days, since the Association closed at 5:00 p.m.

When Dick went to the farmers market, we both got up at 2:00 a.m. to load the berry crates into the truck. I did not go back to bed but started meal preparations for the day, peeling potatoes and making pies or whatever I'd have for dessert. We had a wood-burning stove, so I had to get that started to be ready to make breakfast for the pickers. I woke them up at 5:00 a.m. for breakfast. I had a big pot of coffee ready and lots of bread, cereal, and whatever fruit we had, usually strawberries. Once finished, they grabbed a carrier and went out to pick.

I hurriedly did the dishes so I'd be out by the berry patch when they brought in their first carrier. I had to take the filled boxes out and put them into crates which each held 24 boxes. Then the pickers put empty boxes in the carrier and headed back out to the patch. Dick made the carriers which had a 28" x 12" box attached to four legs about two feet above the ground. This allowed the women to put the berries into the carrier without wasting time and effort bending all the way to the ground. A handle on the carrier allowed for easy movement along the row of raspberries as they picked.

At 11:00 a.m., I'd go in to start lunch. I had a big kettle of potatoes to boil on the wood stove but had to be careful not to get the stove too hot, or the chimney would catch on fire. I'd prepare the meat—beef that I had cold packed (preserved in glass jars) the previous winter, a roast, chicken, or pork. We always had a vegetable from our large garden and, of course, a dessert which I had made earlier in the day. I'd call the pickers for lunch, about 12:45–1:00 p.m. Meantime, Dick had come back from the market, about 11:00 or 12:00 p.m., took a nap for about an hour, and then had lunch. After lunch, I did the dishes so they'd be ready for supper, then back to the raspberry patch. Once Dick came out and started crating, I'd go and pick. I loved picking raspberries and often picked more than the hired girls.

We picked half the patch one day and the other half the next. When Dick took berries to the market in Minneapolis, we'd work until 7:00 or 8:00 p.m., or until it was too dark. We'd have supper after 8:00 p.m. We ate in the dining room with the table extended. Dick made benches for the sides of the table, and we had chairs at the ends. Again, we'd have potatoes, mashed or riced, bacon, ham, or hotdogs for meat, and lots of bread, butter, and cheese. We had milk cows, so when the milkman came in the morning to pick up the milk, he'd bring butter and big chunks of cheese. After supper, I'd ask the girls if they'd help dry the dishes. I always washed and rinsed them. Some girls helped, and others said they did not come here to do dishes! A few went to help Dick and the hired man milk the cows. Many had come from farms and enjoyed the farm environment.

The girls all came from the Bohemian communities of Montgomery or New Prague, and all spoke English. They wore dresses or skirts and blouses, no slacks or shorts at that time, and they all had straw hats but not sunbonnets like mine. We did not pick on Saturdays, and the girls looked forward to going into Minneapolis to shop. They'd walk to the Glen Lake Sanatorium, about a mile away, and catch the bus from there into town. On weekdays, when finished picking, they played the old phonograph on the porch, go swimming, or just horse around and have water fights by the outside water pump. They liked to tease the hired man and when he was out cultivating near the raspberry patch, they'd yell "whoa," and his horse would stop. They all had a good laugh.

Raspberries took a lot of care. They had to be covered in the winter by bending the canes and plowing dirt over them. In the spring, we carefully uncovered them, pulling the soil away with a hoe. The old canes, which bore the previous year, had to be cut at the bottom and pulled away from the new canes, which were then tied to the stake. I didn't mind that, but there were so many and it bothered my hands so that in the morning my fingers would be all swollen and it was 11:00 a.m. before they got limbered up. That's what started my arthritis. The tops of the canes had to be cut off, and some of the bushes were like little trees, so that was very hard. All 8,379 bushes had to be hoed to keep the soil loose and weed-free. Both Dick and I spent much of the spring with this work to get the raspberries to the point of bearing. We had two kinds: Lathams, also called Four's, and Kings, which were a little smaller but sweeter.

For nine years, our income came mainly from raspberries and the few dairy cows that we had, but then the Depression hit. A few years into the Depression, it no longer paid to have raspberries. The price dropped to $1.30 a crate. We paid the berry pickers $0.48 a crate plus room and board. The empty crate and boxes cost $0.24. There were times when no one bought the berries.

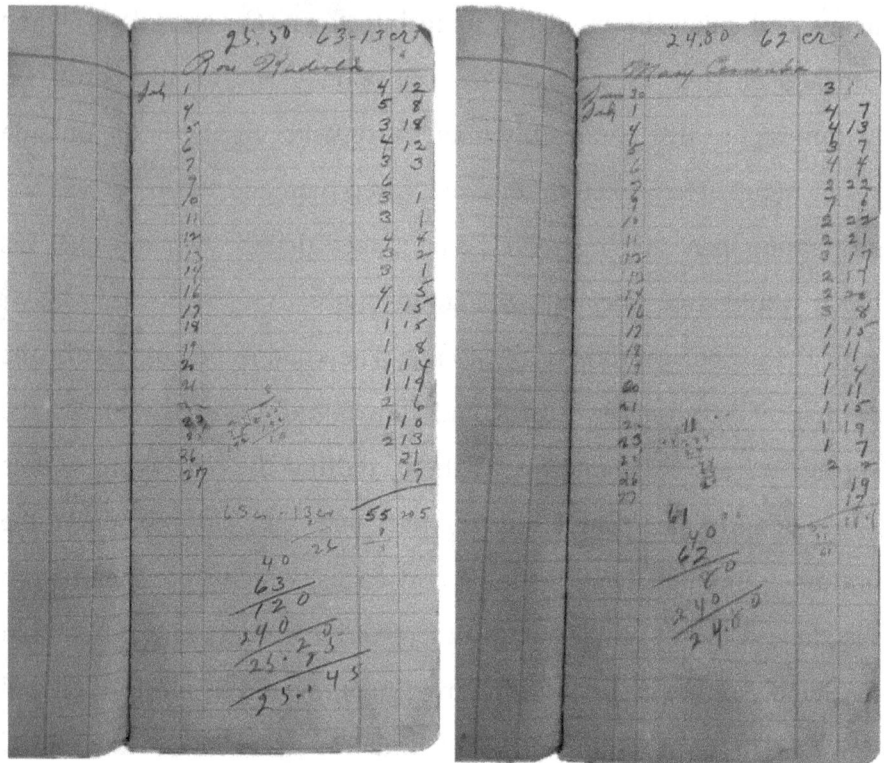

Example of record kept for berry pickers.

To make matters worse, dry weather and windstorms hurt the crop in 1933. Hoping for a change in weather in 1934, we uncovered, cleaned out, and tied the berries in March of that year. In April and May, the weather was hot and dry with temperatures over 100 degrees, scorching and shriveling up the raspberry bushes. By mid-May, we realized the bushes were too far gone to produce fruit, so we pulled out the stakes, and Dick plowed the bushes under on May 21 and 22, 1934.

The following newspaper accounts support the importance of the raspberry crop to area growers and how it put the town of Hopkins on the map.

The Excelsior Fruit Growers Association started in 1900 as a cooperative with about 100 Hopkins area growers (the Holasek family being one). The Association marketed fruit and shipped berries around the country. In 1929, it shipped 26 carloads of berries. Each carload had 850 crates and each crate had 24 pints of berries!

But the Depression and drought threatened continued raspberry production. Weather conditions only got worse in 1934. Dry weather and unprecedented heat destroyed crops. Winter wheat and alfalfa crops were lost. Seed could not germinate due to the dust storms and the high winds which swept away the topsoil. Cows ate leaves off trees, which replaced the hay that didn't exist. Pasturelands dried up. The strawberry crop which comes in May and June yielded only 2–5% of normal production. In May, temperatures reached 106 degrees, scorching strawberry fields.

On June 4, rain finally fell, but with it came a terrific wind which cut a narrow path through southern Hennepin County, from Eden Prairie up through Glen Lake. It blew a resident's chicken coop off its foundation and collapsed the south end of his barn, injuring him as he got caught out in the storm. Uprooted trees and broken branches littered the road in Glen Lake. The cyclone-like winds left many raspberry bushes twisted around broken stakes in the wake of the storm. Even though rain had come, the wind left such destruction that many farmers pulled out the stakes and plowed the berry canes under. Predictions for the surviving raspberry crop for other farmers in the area ran as high as 50% as some clung to the hope that there would still be a crop.[33]

Three weeks later, another horrific storm hit the area, killing a farmer in Hamel and injuring cattle in collapsed barns. The drought had a damaging effect on cattle farmers. Lacking feed, the cattle became emaciated, and finally the government stepped in to help. Under the Depression's Agricultural Adjustment Act (AAA), officials appraised cattle. The diseased or emaciated animals were disposed of on the farms, and those fit for food were shipped out for slaughter.[34]

The importance of the raspberry crop to the local economy did not go unnoticed, and it was clear that farmers could not continue with the price at $1.30 to $1.50 a crate. Somehow the demand for berries had to increase, which would raise the price. Art Plankers, manager of the Red Owl grocery store in Hopkins, and James Markham, editor of the *Hennepin County Review*, came up with a plan. They decided to celebrate the raspberry crop with a designated "raspberry day." In 11 days and with only $350, an annual Raspberry Day was declared. Businesses got on board: Peterson Dairy donated cream for raspberries, and Chaska Sugar Beets donated 100 pounds of sugar. Minneapolis mayor Tom Latimer urged all residents to "Motor to Hopkins for Raspberry Day." Twenty thousand people came to devour 7,000 dishes of raspberries with sugar and cream. Farmers sold crates of berries on

First Raspberry Festival Parade, 1935. Courtesy of the Hopkins Historical Society (HHS2007.36.10-P).

the street for $3 which allowed them to survive the Depression. This began the annual tradition of the Raspberry Festival—still celebrated today—and gained national attention when the Raspberry Festival Queen, Beatrice Bella "BeBe" Shopp, from Hopkins, became Miss America in 1948.[35]

6. LIFE IN THE 1930s

Farm work continued year round; some chores being left for after berry season. Once we no longer had berries for income, we gradually increased our herd of milk cows from 8 to 20. We had 90–100 chickens and sold eggs to relatives and neighbors. Lilliard and Dick worked together on everything from mending farm machinery to helping each other with the annual butchering of a cow and pig. The brothers had a close bond since childhood.

Lilliard inherited the farm of his father John when he retired and moved there in 1928 when he married Aimee M. Matchke from a Czech family in Hopkins.

We had the adjacent farm of Uncle Steve's. Dick and I enjoyed good times with Lilliard and Aimee at dances, parties, and family gatherings. On retiring from their farm, John and Mary Holasek moved to a house they bought in Hopkins.

Automobiles were becoming more common in the late 1920s, and the horse and buggies had to share the roads. Most people still used a horse and buggy for short distances to go shopping or to church. Horns startled the horses, often causing runaways and serious accidents. The narrow dirt roads became slippery after rain, and deep ruts developed with people getting stuck. Our neighbors, the Pichas, tipped over with their horse and buggy right in front of our house, so Dick went and helped them out.

Lilliard and Aimee (Matchke) Holasek's wedding photo, December 6, 1928.

Holasek family gathering, Mary and John standing, front row left to right: Aimee, Lilliard (with accordion), Hazel, Richard, Evelyn.

An evening out, left to right: Evelyn, Richard, Aimee, Lilliard.

We bought our first car for $975 around 1925, a Dodge, noted for its high clearance and ability to plow through snowdrifts and muddy roads. Dick had driven his father's car, a big Velie, and also drove his Uncle Joe's car, a Dodge. Once, we got stuck with the car on the way back from a show at night. We had no light except for a lantern. Dick left me in the car and went to get the team of horses to pull the car out of the deep ruts. He hitched them up to the car and drove them while I steered the car. We finally got the car out, but the lantern spooked the horses, and they went wild. Dick unhooked them from the car and told me to take the team back to the barn. They ran so fast that I stumbled over a harrow in the dark and barely hung

Dishes from Richard and Evelyn's 12-piece place setting used on special occasions.

onto them until they finally reached the barn. They then tried to get into their stalls, harness and all, and I tried to hold them back until Dick came with the car and got them unhooked and into the barn. What a terrible, terrible night, pitch dark and no electricity, just the lantern.

Kerosene lantern used on Holasek farm before electricity.

Radios became affordable in the 1930s, and we purchased our first one on December 10, 1931. They ran on two AA batteries which cost between $3 and $4. Batteries didn't last long, and I'd get new ones at Kokesh Hardware.[36] The radio allowed us to keep up with the news and weather in addition to listening to entertaining serial radio programs. Once we got electricity in 1935, we replaced the battery-run radio with one run by electricity. Dick built a shelf for it in the kitchen, and we rarely missed our favorite newscaster Cedric Adams with his daily news program on WCCO. The other station we often listened to was KSTP.

We had a lot of land that had to be cleared of trees so it could be used for crops. During the Depression, men came and asked for work, so Dick let them cut the trees and take the wood to heat their homes. If we needed to hire men to grub out stumps or do other field work, we didn't have to advertise in the paper, but asked friends who knew who was looking for work. Our first hired man had gone to school with Dick, and we had him off and on. Later, a neighbor had a hired man, and when she no longer needed him, he came and worked for us and stayed with us. At times, we had eight to ten men working in fields nearby. Also, at that time, 62nd Street went through. We could see the men working their way through a hill with picks and shovels, and they built fires to keep themselves warm. It was a cold winter, but the men at least had a job.

Despite the Depression, Dick and I went out in the evenings with Lilliard and Aimee for dinner in Minneapolis or dances at the ZCBJ Bohemian Hall in Glen Lake. When together with Lilliard and

Aimee one evening in the summer of 1934, Lilliard lifted his pant legs and said, "Look how swollen my ankles are." He began feeling tired and ill, taking to bed on August 27, 1934. His health continued to deteriorate, and he spent a week in St. Mary's Hospital before his death on October 13, 1934, of Bright's disease, a kidney disease. He was only 31. Aimee eventually sold the farm and auctioned off the farm equipment on March 21, 1935. Aimee remarried and had 4 sons and 14 grandchildren by the time she died in May 1978 at 73 years.

We all were in shock. Dick never recovered from the loss of his best friend and brother. They had worked together on their farms, repairing machinery, butchering cows and hogs, tending raspberries, and now Dick was alone. Over the next several years, I'd see Dick go around just shaking his head. He rarely talked about it but once said, "Sometimes things happen, and you never know why." But I know something inside of him died with Lilliard. They had been so close and this plus Uncle Steve's death ten years earlier, and simmering problems with Nettie caused him to brood. He lost his sense of humor and fun-loving nature and, at times, drank too much. Now that Lilliard was gone, so too were the good times we had at dances, going into Minneapolis for dinner, and joking around with family and friends. My role on the farm changed too, as I now helped with many of the outdoor chores that Lilliard would have done. Sometimes, Dick went out and didn't come home until late in the evening or early the next morning, and I had to milk the cows.

Added to this loss came Dick's father John who died in his sleep, apparently of a heart attack in November 1936. He was 72. My mother Petrolina died suddenly in July 1939. She had been hanging wallpaper in their house and, one evening, complained of her arms hurting. Everyone thought it was from her working with the wallpaper, but it was a sign of a coming heart attack. She died a few days later. She was only 61 years old. It was a terrible shock to our family.

One great improvement came in January 1935 when electric lines from Northern States Power reached our farm. Before that, we had kerosene lanterns and lamps, but Dick didn't like using them all the time, so he put in a battery-run electric plant for lights only, but it was not strong enough for things like ironing. On the first night that we had electricity, Dick said to turn on all the lights, and we drove down to the main road, turned around, and came back toward the house to see what it looked like. We did that several times. It was the most amazing thing to see the house lit up with such bright lights that could be seen from such a distance. The next night, my parents came, and we told them we were celebrating getting electricity![37]

We had a telephone for a couple of years, but it was unreliable, and the phone company stopped service when winds kept knocking down the lines. Our neighbors Winfred and Dell Eckert had a phone and, for years, I walked to their house when we needed to use a phone.

Another major change came when we decided to start a family. I became pregnant in March 1937. I had a fairly normal pregnancy. My parents gave me a baby shower on November 14. Early on November 27, we had a snowstorm, and I started having labor pains at 5 a.m. So Dick and our hired man Jense had to plow the road around the house to allow Dick to get me to my folks in

Hopkins. Once plowed, they weighted down the back of the truck so it wouldn't skid on the icy road, and Dick made it to Hopkins. My sister Gloria's husband Norman drove me to St. Barnabas Hospital in Minneapolis, and I remember having labor pains all the way. Dorothy entered the world the next day, November 28, at 11:00 a.m.

While I had been working side by side with Dick in the field as well as milking cows, I now needed to stay indoors. We then had a series of hired men to take my place. We occasionally had a hired man before for short periods of time, but now it was a regular practice.

The birth of our second child Janet posed a more difficult problem. At some point during my pregnancy, I suddenly wasn't able to keep food down. This continued for two weeks. Finally, Doctor Kucera said that if I couldn't keep food down the next day or two, the baby had to be taken rather than risk my life. The next day, I was overjoyed when my breakfast stayed down, and I had no more problems during my pregnancy.

However, on November 11, 1940, there was a terrific snowstorm which buried the state in snow. The day started out warm and balmy, so people went to work without coats. By 5:00 p.m., as people headed home from work, they had to push through snowdrifts in blinding snow. I was eight months pregnant and was working in the barn, not realizing how the weather had changed. I could barely see in front of me as I made my way to the house in blowing snow and up the icy front steps, but made it safely!

One month later, Dick took me to my folks' house in Hopkins, and Norman drove me to St. Barnabas Hospital in

Richard and Evelyn with children Janet and Dorothy, c. 1941.

Evelyn holding Dorothy and Janet (left), Dorothy and Janet (right), 1941.

Minneapolis. Janet entered the world at 11:43 a.m. on December 16, 1940. While Dorothy was blonde and blue eyed with very fair skin, Janet had dark brown eyes and almost black hair.

Author's Notes

My mother never talked much about World War II, and I was too young to understand how it impacted us. Congress had passed the Selective Training and Service Act in September 1940, requiring all men between the ages of 21 and 45 to register with their local draft board. This was the nation's first peacetime draft. After the Japanese attacked Pearl Harbor on December 7, 1941, Congress amended the above Act to require all able-bodied men between the ages of 18 and 64 to register. At that time, Daddy was 40 years old, and he registered with Local Board No. 24, Hennepin County, at the Town Hall in Excelsior, Minnesota. Periodically, Daddy would receive a Notice of Classification. I have found four of these along with partially used ration coupon books from the war years. Daddy's classification number changed over the years, but he always had deferred status because men 38 and over were not being drafted, and he was in agriculture, an occupation necessary to feed the troops during the war. One of my first memories as a child—I must have been about three or four years old—came when Daddy showed me his draft card and explained that his 4A classification meant he would not have to serve because of his age and occupation, except under an extreme emergency.

Richard's War Classification, 1943.

During the war years, Mother kept busy tending to Dorothy and me. Daddy was able to get hired help—which was especially needed in the summer for planting and harvesting—by finding men who were older than the draft age. The war affected everyone in the family in some way. All four of us had a War Ration Book that limited the number or amount of rationed items we could purchase. These items included sugar, gasoline, tires, canned goods, beef, coffee, and shoes, to mention a few. If purchasing gasoline, Daddy had to prove that it would be used for farm chores and not for pleasure riding. Among the women, sugar was the most valuable rationed item because it was a necessary ingredient in canning fruit. I found a form that Mother filled out indicating how many quarts of fruit she would can in 1942. Rationing regulations provided one pound of sugar for every four quarts of canned fruit. In 1942, she estimated that she would can 36 quarts of apricots, 45 quarts of pears, 60 quarts of peaches, 15 quarts of plums, and 12 quarts of cherries. She was granted the requisite amount of sugar for this and promised to make a written itemized report to the Board before December 1, 1942.

I remember conversations among the farm women regarding how much sugar each planned to use. They often told stories about how some women cheated to get more sugar than they needed and would then sell it. Others told about women hiding bags of sugar under floorboards only to find it hard as a rock several months later, when they planned to use or sell it.

Nylon hose was another item in short supply. Mother loaned her single pair of nylon hose to her sister Gloria, who needed them to go to a wedding, and Gloria returned them to Mother in a box so they wouldn't snag.

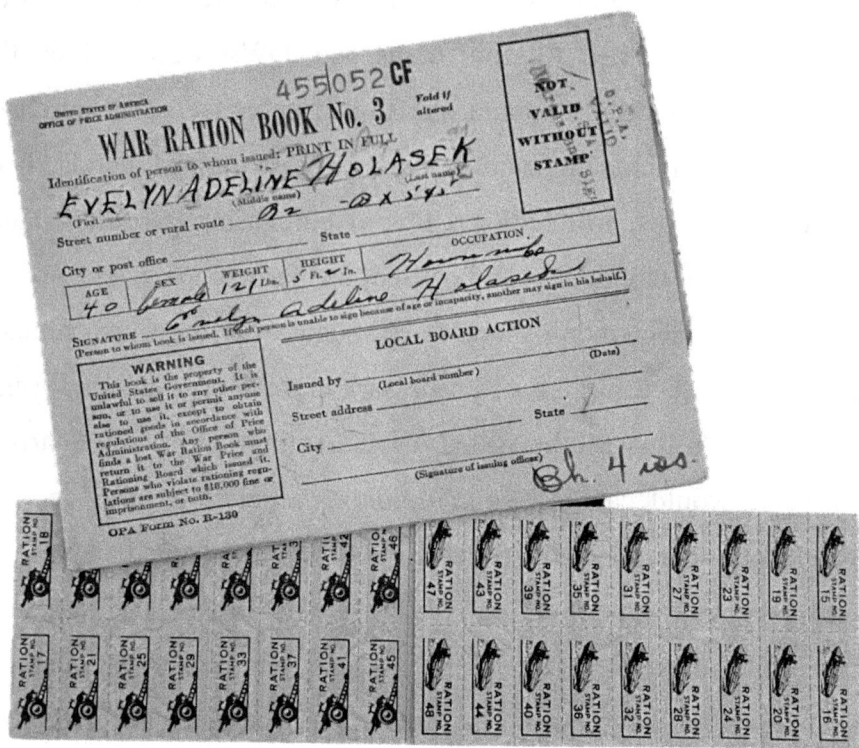

Evelyn's War Ration Book.

Janet's Certificate of Registrar for war ration stamps, May 5, 1942.

People were urged to show their patriotism by buying war bonds to help pay for the war. Daddy's records show that in 1941, he purchased $1,500 in bonds, $2,062.50 in 1942, and $937.50 in 1943. This must have been a strain on my parents given what little income they made. In 1943, Congress passed a Victory Tax which had to be paid with the annual income tax. President Roosevelt asked for 5% on income, but Congress reduced it to 3%. This tax lasted for just 1943.

While I was too young to remember, I am certain that my parents listened to the news regularly on the radio and followed the war's progress in the *Minneapolis Tribune,* which they got daily. They both paid attention to the political scene, voted at every election, and felt it their privilege and duty to be responsible citizens.

7. HIRED HELP

Farm work kept the whole family busy year round. When we had raspberries in the 1920s and 1930s, sometimes we had a hired man to help with the milking during the peak of the raspberry season. At times, field work required that we have a hired man. After Lilliard died, we also needed help, as Lilliard and Dick had done so much work together.

One of the men we had for a while, we called Montana Jack. That's the only name we knew him by. In the late 1930s, we had a man called Jense. Again, that's all we ever called him and the only name we knew, Jense. He was the one who helped out when Dorothy was born.[38]

Another hired man, Frank, was an alcoholic. Every Saturday, he went to town and never came back in the same clothes. I guess he spent his money, and then had to trade his clothes to get more money for drinks. He had a beautiful, probably very expensive, violin but needed money for alcohol, so I offered him $10 for it. We didn't have the money, but I told my dad about the violin, and he gave me $10 to buy it. Eventually, Dick had had it with Frank's drinking and one day, when we were working in the field, Dick told me to go home, and pay Frank, and tell him that he was through. So I did what Dick asked and, after I told Frank he had to leave, he asked, "Why doesn't Dick come and tell me himself?" I said, "You'll have to go ask him!" Dick didn't like confrontations.

I still had the violin and, later, got a letter from Frank asking me to send it. Dick had seen the violin and asked where I got it and was not happy when I told him I bought it for $10. I told him that my dad had given me the money. Frank no doubt knew the value of the violin and in his letter, was quite insistent that I send it, even though I had paid him for it. There seemed to be the potential for trouble if I refused to send it, so I wrapped it up carefully and put it in the mail. Eventually, Frank wrote that he had received it and thanked me.

People wonder if I was ever afraid of the hired men, who were sometimes complete strangers in the house, especially when Dick went out to the blacksmith or the hardware store. But times were different then. I never feared them, and we never locked our doors until Dorothy was born.

The best, most trustworthy and faithful hired man we ever had was Ray Carter. Perhaps because he had been an orphan, he appreciated having a home where he felt wanted. He had worked for someone we knew and no longer needed him, so he came to us. He never complained and did whatever work Dick asked him to do. Sometimes, Dick bought a crate of peaches or pears, and I'd have to can them in the evening so they wouldn't spoil. After Dick had gone to bed, Ray would come and sit on the floor in the kitchen while I worked; he was a great talker. I asked him, "Why don't you go to bed?" He said, "I don't want to see you working down here alone."

Later, he joined the army in World War II, and he continued to write us. He went to Hawaii and sent me a chest which must have gotten lost on the way, but he brought us a wooden, carved tiger from Hawaii that I had sitting on our steps in the old house. That's another story. Years later, when I went to visit Janet and her family in Colorado, I came back home to find that the tiger had orange and black stripes painted on it. I asked Dick about it, and he said that he had always wanted to put stripes on it so when I was gone, he just went ahead and painted them!

At some point, Ray got married and, for a while, we lost contact, but then he wrote again and, in June of 1977, came to visit us. That's the last time that we saw him. He was just the most wonderful man. I will never forget him.

At first, the hired men lived in the house with us. Later, they'd help during busy times in the summer but not live in the house. Our income tax returns show how much money we spent for hired help from 1941–1952, as indicated below. Dick always paid the men in cash. He never wrote a check but kept cash and important papers in a metal box in the basement in an unused chimney. The box had a combination number to open it. Dick had removed some bricks from the chimney so he could slip the box in, and then replace the bricks. This was our "safety deposit" box.

MONEY SPENT ON HIRED HELP (1941–1952)

1941: $339.00	1947: $74.00
1942: $126.00	1948: $251.87
1943: $157.50	1949: $303.50
1944: $295.50	1950: $0.00
1945: $121.77	1951: $0.00
1946: $95.00	1952: $180.00

The last hired man we had was David Pinks, who we got by advertising in the newspaper. He lived in St. Paul with his mother who drove him out to see the place where he worked and to ask, "Do you have your own butter?" I thought that a rather curious question, but she seemed satisfied with our house. She apparently wanted a safe place for her son to work in the fresh air during the summer. We got along fine; he was very helpful, and he did some of my chores like going to get the cows from the night pasture at 6:00 a.m. so Dick could milk them. He continued to stay in touch with us and came to visit us several times a year, usually around lunchtime. Dick and I joked that he liked my cooking! Once he came at a crucial time when we were remodeling the barn. He helped us for several days, which was much appreciated. He continued to come well into the 1980s after he was married and had children, but eventually his visits stopped, and we lost touch with him.

8. BUTCHERING

Czech farm families had substantial meals three times a day often with meat as part of all meals. We usually had bacon and eggs for breakfast, preceded by a dish of oatmeal. For noon and evening meals, our meat would be a pork or beef roast, pork chops, or ham, and always potatoes, bread, and a vegetable. Often our meals came from food we raised on the farm. Potatoes and vegetables grown and preserved in the summer and fall lasted throughout the winter. For meat we butchered a cow, calf, and one or two hogs, usually in December or January, the coldest part of the year since we lacked refrigeration until the late 1930s. It was not uncommon for families to butcher three pigs in one day as Dick and Lilliard did in January of 1932. In January 1934, they killed two hogs.

Butchering day meant a full day of hard work. I heated two huge kettles of water on the wood stove then carried the boiling water to a tub outside where Dick had already killed the pig and had it hanging on a pulley and rope on the north side of the house. I poured the water into the tub under the pig, and Dick lowered it into the tub, turning it around and around until the bristles started to come off. Then Dick raised the pig out of the water. I poured out the water, and Dick lowered the pig down into the empty tub. Then, with very sharp knives, we scraped all the bristles off the pig. Once done, the pig was raised again, a fresh bucket placed under it, and Dick gutted the pig letting the intestines, heart, liver, and other parts drop out. Dick caught the blood in a jar, and I kept stirring it; later, we made it into delicious blood sausage. I took the liver inside, washed it, and set it aside for the evening meal. I'd slice and bread it and fry it with onions.

After the insides had come out, Dick cut the pig in half and carried the two halves into the cellarway (the outside entrance to the basement) to cool off over the next two or three days. Then he cut it into roasts, hams, and bacon. My folks used to buy half a hog every winter, and I learned from my mother as she made sausage, pickled pig's feet, and rendered the fat into lard which we used as shortening. My mother fried the smaller pieces of fat into "cracklings" which my dad loved to eat with cornmeal. I fried down the pork just as my mother had, and we always had a five-gallon crock of lard and two crocks of salted-down meat. Before refrigeration, that was the way we preserved meat.

Dick and I made sausage by grinding some of the pork, adding a little cooked rice, and plenty of spices, especially garlic and pepper. We saved all the intestines, which I washed and scraped the inside with a knife to clean them thoroughly. We had a big sausage grinder where I mixed everything, and then attached an intestine to the spout, tying the other end, and then turned the crank until the intestine was filled. We put the sausages on waxed paper on the table in the back porch, which served as a refrigerator, and I could reach the table from a kitchen window. It got so cold that the sausages froze and kept a long time. We also made blood sausage, which was a lot of work but oh, so good! Once the blood sausage was prepared, we put it into the pig's stomach which I had thoroughly cleaned and, if we had extra, we put it into any remaining intestines. They had to be cooked because the blood had to set. Once cooked and thoroughly cooled, I could slice it just like bread and fry it. I can still smell that wonderful aroma of garlic and onions with the blood sausage that Dick and the girls just loved.

Dick loved the small, fried pieces of fat just as my dad had. We called them *skwarke*. Dick also loved the pig's feet. He'd save the part of the foot from the knee down and sit at the kitchen table carefully cleaning between the toes and the entire foot, which he wanted absolutely clean. I'd cook the feet and make a broth with vinegar, salt, and pepper and pour it over the feet. Once cooled, it jelled making those pickled pig's feet that Dick enjoyed for the next several weeks.

The hams went into a brine. Dick had a recipe from his parents for that. The hams and bacon sat in the brine for a certain length of time, and then Dick hung them in our smokehouse way up to the ceiling. He kept a fire at the bottom, and the smoke rose up to cure them. They were very, very good. Our smokehouse sat on the south side of the barn. Nearly every part of the hog was used, including the tongue, liver and, as was commonly said, every part but the squeal!

In the winter, we also butchered a cow. Dick hired Mr. Dvorak to come and help with that. Once again, we carried large pieces into the cellarway to cool for about a week, and then Dick would cut steaks, roasts, boiling meat for soup, etc. The meat had to be kept cold, so we put pieces on the front and back porches and in the snow by the house. I "cold packed" a lot of the meat so we could have it in the summer, when we had berry pickers. To do this, I put chunks of meat into well-washed and sterilized fruit jars, put in a bit of salt, filled the jars with water, sealed them but did not tighten the lids all the way. I had a big boiler with a wire rack that held 11 jars. They had to boil for three and a half hours on the wood stove. When it was time to take them out, I had to close all the doors and windows because there could be no draft when I took them out, or the jars would break. I'd take them out, one by one, very carefully, and then tighten the lid on each one. When we had berry pickers, I'd open two or three jars, slice the meat, and make the most delicious gravy from the broth.

I used to kill chickens as well. There was a place right outside the barn where we had a cement slab and a stump. I'd hold the chicken by its feet with its head across the stump and with a sharp axe chop off the head with one whack. The chicken continued to move wildly so I had to hold it firmly by the feet while blood flew around, and eventually it stopped moving. I dunked it into very hot water and pulled all the feathers off. When Dorothy and Janet were big enough, they'd help take off the feathers. I'd take the chicken inside and cut it open, taking out all the insides, but saving the gizzard, liver, and heart to use in dressing when I baked the chicken. I kept some of the longer feathers, washed them and tied the ends so I could use the feathers to grease the tops of *kolach* and bread. We called this a *stetka* (Czech word for brush). Janet still uses one I made for her.

In the 1940s, there was a place on Excelsior Avenue in Hopkins where we could take half a cow or hog and have it cut up into roasts, steaks, chops, and or ground into hamburger. The individual pieces were wrapped in white freezer paper and frozen.

Evelyn's stetka.

Meat locker on Excelsior Boulevard in Hopkins. Courtesy of the Hopkins Historical Society (HHS2007.40.81).

There, we rented a locker for the meat and, every week, Dick would go and get what we needed. That meant we could have fresh meat, and it was a welcome change from the salted meat. I also no longer had to cold pack.

Finally, in 1948, we bought a 30-cubic foot Amana freezer for $737 which we put in our basement. I now could freeze vegetables and some fruits, a much easier task than canning them. I also had meat available all the time, which helped greatly in planning meals.

9. MAKING HAY, HUSKING CORN, THRESHING

We had about 85 acres of land on our farm with probably 20 of the acres in hay, both alfalfa and a finer hay that grew in a meadow area. The alfalfa field was directly across the main road, Baker Road, from our house, and the meadow hay field was about one mile from the house. We fed hay to the cows and horses, and that made up an important part of their diet in addition to silage. Making hay, that is harvesting it and storing it either in the barn hayloft or in a haystack for winter, usually began in July. Of all the summer work, this was the hottest and dirtiest because of the dust and the loose, prickly hay that would trickle down your back. I always wore a dress, I called it an apron, to keep as cool as possible, while Dick wore his usual farm clothes: overalls with a blue, cotton shirt. We did all of this with horse-drawn equipment. While some farmers had hay loaders which fed the hay into the back of the wagon, and a few had tractor driven hay balers, our farm's size didn't warrant such modern and expensive machinery. After World War II, in the late 1940s and 1950s, farmers saw enormous changes in farming technology. But the new equipment required larger farms while the family farm, like ours, could not afford these expenditures other than to replace horses with a tractor. However, we still harvested hay into the mid-1950s with horse-drawn machinery.

Dick cut the hay with the horse-pulled hay mower then raked

it into windrows and let it dry for a few days. As he cut it, one could see mice scurrying for a new home, grasshoppers flitting about, and an occasional snake trying to find safety. If it rained before we got the hay into the barn, he'd have to turn it over with a pitchfork and wait a few days for it to dry, as damp hay in the hayloft could cause a fire.

We usually "put up" hay in the early afternoon. I watched from the house for Dick to leave the barn with the wagon, grabbed my sunbonnet, and climbed onto the hay wagon as he stopped by the house. When the children were small and couldn't be left alone in the house, they came with us and sat in a shady spot on the edge of the hayfield while we loaded the wagon.

It took 5 to 10 minutes to get to the hayfield. Dick stopped the horses alongside a windrow and the two of us, using pitchforks, would get a forkful of loose hay, lift it over our heads, and throw it onto the wagon taking care to get it around the sides of the wagon while the middle generally took care of itself. It took some skill to have it evenly cover the bottom of the wagon. After the wagon was about half full, I climbed onto the wagon to distribute the hay and stomp it down while Dick continued to pitch hay into the wagon until it was full. If we had a hired man, both he and Dick pitched the hay while I stomped. We had to be careful to fill the wagon evenly and not to pile it too high, or hay would slide off on the way home. The only part I didn't like was lifting a pile of hay with my pitchfork and having snakes fall out onto me. The field mice and insects didn't bother me except for the horse-flies and boy, could they bite!

Richard pitching hay from horse-drawn hayrack to top of haystack where Evelyn is spreading it to keep the haystack even. Note ladder on left side for Evelyn to climb onto the haystack, 1950s.

The best part was riding home on top of the wagon. Sitting on top of the wagon, I felt a bit of a breeze and could see for what seemed like miles. I did have a scare one time when we had taken the girls and had them sit nearby in a shaded area. I was stomping hay and just happened to look up and saw little Janet walking toward the road. I have no idea why she got up and left Dorothy, but I frantically climbed down from the wagon and ran after her, calling her name. Thankfully, I caught up with her just before she reached the busy Baker Road! I walked her back to where Dorothy was sitting and explained why she had to stay there.

Once we finished loading the wagon, Dick drove it as close as possible to the north side of the barn, unhooked the horses, and drove them through the barn to the south side where I took control of them. Back on the hay wagon, Dick swung the giant hay mow door down, which opened up the side of the barn leading into the hayloft. Using a rope which dropped down from inside the hayloft, he let down a giant fork that ran on an iron track on the inside roof of the barn, onto the top of the loose hay in the wagon. He sank the fork into the hay. The horses were attached to a pulley and rope connected to the giant forkful of hay. When the girls were older, one of them sat under a tree near Dick, and he called out when the hay was ready to be lifted into the hayloft.

Then one of the girls rang a loud bell that told me it was time to drive the horses forward to pull the hay into the loft. I called "giddyup," and the horses went forward. The rope, by means of pulleys, pulled the forkful of hay up and along the track into the hayloft. When the horses had gone as far as they could, Dick yanked the rope attached to the forkful of hay, and it dropped the loose hay onto the hayloft floor. I turned the horses around and positioned myself to be ready for the next ring of the bell. Each hay wagon had about 12 of these gigantic forkfuls of hay. Later, Dick climbed up the barn's inside ladder to the hay mow and spread the hay evenly on the floor. If any was damp, he made sure to spread it carefully as damp hay can cause a fire by spontaneous combustion and, occasionally, a barn has burned down from this. The girls took turns ringing the bell and always had a book with them.

Once the hayloft was filled, or when we had poorer quality hay, we built a haystack close to the barn and covered it with a tarp.

The importance of hay as a major source of food and nutrients for milk cows cannot be underestimated. Every day, Dick filled their mangers with hay, first throwing it down from the hayloft to the barn's main floor and through a chute into the lower cow barn. He then went and distributed it in the cows' feeding mangers.

We had a few acres of land a mile or so from the farm where meadow hay grew and was gathered in early September. The ground was marshy and cool, and the hay much finer and smoother than alfalfa. We used it in the chicken nests and between the rows of strawberries which made picking the berries easier. Dick cut and raked the hay into piles and, at times in the 1950s, we used the tractor to pull the wagon. It was one of the few times Janet drove the tractor while Dick and I, using pitchforks, threw the hay into the wagon. Once back home, the hay went into the hayloft, but was kept separate from the coarser, scratchy alfalfa.

We grew several acres of corn, some for silage for the milk cows and some to shell and grind for animal food. Our silo was attached to the barn, and there was a ladder on the outside of it as well as in the basement of the barn. Harvesting corn for silage usually began in late August. Dick put up the pipes leading from about eight feet above ground to the top of, and into, the silo. He had already cut the corn and with the horse drawn wagon went into the field and loaded the corn stalks onto the wagon. He drove the wagon back near the silo where he threw the corn stalks with their green ears into a machine which chopped them up and blew the pieces into the pipe up to the top and into the silo. It was now called silage.

My job was to be in the silo and distribute the chopped corn pieces as they came down the big pipe inside the silo. The pipe had a rope attached to it which I used to swing the pipe around to distribute the incoming silage evenly. I also had to stomp on the corn pieces to pack them and get all the air out or the silage would spoil. The silo filled up gradually from the bottom to the top. As it filled, I had to enter the silo by climbing a ladder on the exterior of the silo, which was on the part of the silo that was inside the barn's basement. By the time the silo was filled near the top, I had quite a climb up and down the ladder.

I remember one time when it was almost to the top and Dick was putting in the last load, as I climbed the ladder and over the edge into the silo, I felt something bite my leg several times. I looked and there, inside the silo, was a nest of wasps. My leg started to go numb, and I thought I should get down, but then the silage started coming and knocked the wasps down and away from my leg. Frightened that they'd start stinging me again, I managed to distribute the silage, and fortunately enough wasps were struck down by the silage so that I could climb out and down the ladder safely, even with a numb leg. That evening, Dick went up into the silo and burned the wasp nest. Silos could be dangerous. You could slip and fall, and it was a long way down to a cement floor. During the winter, either Dick or I climbed up into the silo from the inside of the barn and pitched forkfuls of silage down so that it could be put into the cows' mangers, along with hay, as their feed. By the end of the winter, we had used most of the silage.

An example of a silo being filled through a pipe. Barn and silo on Anton Weber's farm, Tompkins County, New York, 1937, photo by Arthur Rothstein. Courtesy of the Library of Congress, Prints & Photographs Division (fsa-8a08948).

Several acres of corn that were not used for silage were allowed to ripen and had to be husked and stored. Later, we shelled it and ground it as feed for the animals, including the chickens.

Dick had a machine that cut the corn and tied the stalks into bundles. He then "shocked" the bundles into what looked like little wigwams. Once it was dry, Dick and I spent close to two months or so husking it. We started early in the morning and worked until dusk. We'd drive out to the cornfield in our pickup truck. We started by lying several bundles on the ground. We sat on one bunch, and we'd have another bunch in front of us to husk. We each had our own two bundles. When finished, we moved on to the next "wigwam" of shocked bundles. We used a metal husking pin to help strip the corn husks off the ear. Then we snapped the ear of corn off its stem and

Cornfield on Holasek farm with wood pile in distance c. 1940s.

threw the ear into a bucket. When the bucket was filled, we dumped it in the back of our pickup truck and started to fill the bucket again. At noon we drove home, unloaded the truck, had lunch, and went back to husk until dusk. We stored the husked ears of corn in a corn crib attached to our granary near the barn. The corn crib sat above the ground and had slats for sides to allow the corn to get air. It sat above the ground so rodents wouldn't get into it and eat the corn.

Dick and I husked all the corn by hand, a long and tedious process lasting well into the fall after the weather turned cold. We usually started by mid-September and finished in the first weeks of November. My diaries have a few dates. In 1935, we finished husking on November 8. In 1951, we started on September 16 and in 1952, we finished on October 22.

Husking corn was probably the hardest job for me. I had arthritis in my hands, and husking corn made it worse. The ears were large, and the corn kernels were hard and even though we wore gloves, the constant repetition of grabbing the ears and breaking them off the stems hurt my hands. By the time we finished, the weather could be quite cold and there could even be snow on the ground.

One tragic accident happened when our neighboring relative Bill Holasek was out husking with his family in October 1935. A storm came, and it started to rain, so they got in the truck and headed home. They had to cross a little bridge over a creek and just as they crossed it, lightning struck. It hit their daughter Mabel and killed her instantly, shredding her clothes and body. Her brother Joey, sitting next to her, lost some of his hearing but otherwise was not affected. Another daughter in the back of the truck got burned on her back but recovered. The creek might have attracted the lightning as they went over it, but Mabel apparently still had her metal husking pin in her hand which might have attracted the lightning. It was such a tragedy to have such a wonderful, young woman killed returning home after working in the field.

When Dorothy and Janet were too young to be in school, we took them with us into the cornfield. They brought their crayons, pencils, and books and stayed in the truck while we husked. In the morning before going out, I heated bricks in the oven and put them on the floor in the truck so the girls could keep their feet warm.

One year, when we started husking, David Pinks, the 16-year-old hired man, was still with us. He looked at the huge field of

Evelyn's corn husking pin, worn over glove.

corn and said, "Do we have to husk all of this?" You could just see the relief on his face when he knew that he'd soon be leaving to go back home and to school.

During the winter, we shelled the husked corn and fed it to the cows and chickens. We had a hand crank corn sheller in the barn, and I'd haul buckets of corn from the outside corn crib into the barn to shell. I dumped the corn into a slanted tray that fed it into the body of the corn sheller. By turning the hand crank, the corn kernels were stripped from the cob and went into a pail at the bottom of the sheller, and the cobs shot out the side. I brought the corncobs into the house to start a fire in our wood-burning stove and to use as fuel. Turning the crank was hard work, and I spent a lot of time shelling corn this way. Sometimes, Janet came to watch. She liked seeing the corn cobs shoot out the side! Eventually we bought a sheller that was run by the tractor, a great relief to me.

Threshing, the harvesting of oats, involved several farmers going from farm to farm working as a team because of the expense of a threshing machine. The combine later replaced the threshing machine. A farmer's crop could usually be threshed in one day. First, the oats had to be cut with a reaper-binder. This horse-drawn machine cut, bunched, and tied the grain into bundles. Once the field was cut, Dick gathered several of the bundles or sheaves and stood them in a teepee type arrangement to dry. This was known as shocking oats. On our threshing day, the farmers would gather and haul the grain bundles to the threshing machine which separated the grain from the chaff or straw. Oats would be stored in our granary and fed to the animals while the straw would be stored loose or baled and go into the barn to be used as bedding for the horses and cows and, later, the chickens.

My job on threshing day was to feed the farmers. When the girls were old enough, they helped by peeling vegetables. We'd put several leaves in the dining room table to seat everyone. I always made chicken or beef with gravy, mashed potatoes, a vegetable, homemade bread, and apple or blueberry pie for dessert. I usually did this myself, but one year, they changed the schedule in the morning, so Bill Holasek's wife Hattie sent two of their daughters over to help me. Between the three of us, we killed the chickens and chilled them, baked the pies, and got the vegetables ready. It made me terribly nervous to have to rush so much, but that's the way it was, and we had a nice meal for the men. Women took great pride in their providing a hearty meal for the threshing crew.

Threshing on the Holasek farm, 1954.

10. DAIRY YEARS

As of 1934, our sole source of income came from our dairy cows. For years Dick and I milked the cows by hand, but once Dorothy was born, I had to stay in the house, so Dick and a hired man did the milking. In the 1940s, Dick bought two Surge milk machines which made milking a lot easier and faster for him. The Surge machine was a five-gallon, stainless steel bucket with a hose attached to rubber lined suction cups that clamped onto the cows' teats. Once it had finished milking the cow, Dick poured the milk from the Surge bucket into a pail and carried it upstairs to a room in the barn we called the milk house. There, he poured it into milk cans which sat in a cold-water cooler, also a Surge product. Every morning, a truck came to pick up the full cans and leave empty ones. The driver of the milk truck was someone from the area and if Dick was there when he came, they chatted about the weather and crops.

We sold the milk to the Twin City Milk Producers Association, a marketing cooperative started in St. Paul in 1915 by dairy farmers. We had Jersey cows which produced rich milk, and Dick got several awards for our high-quality milk.

We kept some milk for our use, but I always pasteurized it to destroy any harmful bacteria. I had an electric pasteurizer sitting on a chair in the kitchen. It heated the milk to a certain temperature. I never let anyone, especially the girls, drink unpasteurized milk. Dick also would leave some milk in a saucer in the barn for the barn cats.

Milk can used by Richard, marked with his Twin City Milk Producers Association membership number 11.

F.1B T.C.M.P.A. 10-44

RICHARD HOLASEK
ROUTE 2
HOPKINS, MINN.

77
12
P-8-222

AGREEMENT

AGREEMENT, made this _11th_ day of _Dec._, 19_44_, between Twin City Milk Producers Association, a non-profit Minnesota cooperative corporation, hereinafter called Association, and _Richard Holasek_, of the Township of _Eden Prairie_, County of _Hennepin_, and State of Minnesota, hereinafter called Producer, WITNESSETH:

Producer is the owner of _16_ (_16_) dairy cows, is a member of Association and wishes to have the milk and cream produced from cows owned or controlled by him sold and disposed of by and through the Association on a cooperative basis.

In consideration of the mutual covenants herein set forth, the parties hereto mutually promise and agree as follows:

Producer agrees to consign to Association, for sale or disposal for his account as hereinafter provided, all milk and cream hereafter produced by or from cows owned or controlled by him, except such part thereof as may be required by Producer for his home or farm and such as is sold by him at retail. Such milk and cream shall be delivered by Producer at such place or places as may be designated by Association, and when so delivered shall be in a pure and unadulterated state and suitable for sale in the Cities of St. Paul, Minneapolis and adjacent markets.

Association agrees to receive and sell as soon as practicable all milk and cream consigned to it by Producer, or to manufacture the same and sell the products thereof in such manner as it deems to be most advantageous to Producer and its other members. As soon as reasonably possible after the end of each calendar month Association will remit to Producer the average price received by it (including in determining such average price the inventory value of products manufactured during the month and unsold at the end of the month) for all milk and cream handled by it, with appropriate adjustments for quality, grade and location of the farm where the milk or cream is produced. If after a monthly remittance is made funds or charges are received or accrued which were not included in determining the amount of such remittance but which properly should have been included, the same shall be allocated to Producer's Capital Account Ledger on a patronage basis and distributed as outlined below.

Association is authorized to deduct from the proceeds received for milk and cream delivered by Producer and for the products derived therefrom, for the purpose of meeting operating and maintenance expenses of the Association and providing it with adequate capital, such amounts on a patronage basis as the Board of Directors may from time to time determine are necessary and fair and equitable to all patrons delivering milk or cream to the Association. All such deductions made by the Association for the purpose of providing it with capital (except those herein authorized, if any, for the purchase of capital stock) shall be allocated annually to Producer's Capital Account Ledger. Producer's capital account net credits shall be returned to Producer in cash or securities of the Association at such time or times as the Board of Directors of Association may determine; provided that the net amount credited to Producer at the end of each calendar year shall be returned to him within eleven (11) years after the end of each year.

This contract shall be self-renewing for periods of one year each, unless either party shall notify the other in writing not less than thirty (30) days prior to June 1 of any year, beginning with the year _1945_, of his or its intention to terminate the same on the first day of June following such notice.

In case either party fails to perform his or its covenants as herein provided, the party in default shall and will pay to the other, as and for liquidated or stipulated damages, and not as a penalty for his or its breach, the sum of Five Dollars ($5.00) for each cow owned by Producer as hereinabove stated.

IN TESTIMONY WHEREOF, said parties have hereunto set their hands and seals the day and year first above written.

Signed, Sealed and Delivered in the Presence of:

Witness for Association _____

Witness for Producer _____

Twin City Milk Producers Association

By _N.W. Collis_

Richard Holasek
Milk Producer Sign Here.

Richard's contract with Twin City Milk Producers Association.

A CO-OPERATIVE ASSOCIA-
TION OF OVER 7300 DAIRY-
MEN LIVING WITHIN 40
MILES OF THE TWIN CITIES.

EXECUTIVE COMMITTEE
W. S. MOSCRIP, PRES.   LAKE ELMO, MINN.
R. B. GOODHUE, 1ST VICE PRES. DENNISON, MINN.
S. R. HOULTON, 2ND VICE PRES. ELK RIVER, MINN.
FRED M. ROHE, SEC'Y & TREAS.   OSSEO, MINN.
A. T. FRANK   ANOKA, MINN.
H. R. LEONARD
GENERAL MANAGER

TWIN CITY MILK PRODUCERS ASSOCIATION

GENERAL OFFICE
PHONE: NESTOR 2854
2402 UNIVERSITY AVENUE
ST PAUL MINNESOTA

November 5, 1943

Mr. Richard Holasek,
Hopkins, Rt. 2,
Minn.

Dear Mr. Holasek:

        This year our officers decided to determine how many members had had a perfect sanitation record for the year and to write a letter of appreciation to those falling into this group.

        Out of about 6,000 shippers, we found there were 319 who have had a perfect record in both sediment and bacteria from January 1 to November 1 of this year, and you were one of this group. A very large number had just one 2X count or one unsatisfactory sediment pad, but it really means a lot for any shipper to be in the group that did not have a single slip for the entire year.

        We hope you will be coming to the Annual Meeting as we are going to ask those in attendance who have received this letter to stand up and show themselves at the meeting. Furthermore, we are reserving one of our TCMPA Farm Account Books for you and will have these books at the meeting reserved for those presenting this letter. Ask for your copy!

        You will soon receive the annual meeting notice with full particulars about the meeting, and we certainly hope you will make a special effort to be here this year.

        Again, in behalf of the Board of Directors and officers, we wish to express our appreciation of the fine record you have made.

FACTORIES
ALBERTVILLE
ANOKA
CANNON FALLS
CENTERVILLE
DENNISON
ELK RIVER
FARMINGTON
FOREST LAKE
LAKE ELMO
MINNEAPOLIS
NORTHFIELD
ST. PAUL

PRODUCTS
MILK
CREAM
BUTTER
CHEESE
DRY MILK
ICE CREAM MIX
COTTAGE CHEESE
CONDENSED MILK

Very truly yours,
TWIN CITY MILK PRODUCERS ASS'N

H. R. Leonard
Manager

HRLeonard
lrf

Twin City Milk Producers Association's letter to Richard commending his perfect sanitation record and inviting him to the Annual Meeting to be recognized, 1943.

AWARD OF MERIT

By QUALITY CONTROL COMMITTEE, To

Richard Holasek

We are happy to inform you that the Quality Control Committee, in charge of the laboratory testing of milk in this area finds that you have had a PERFECT QUALITY RECORD for the year 1944.

In recognition of this, the Committee has directed that you be given a statement of this achievement and a pin which you can wear showing that you have received such an Award. There were only eight and a half per cent of the shippers who achieved this goal and the Committee heartily congratulates you and members of your family who helped to make this excellent record possible.

In doing this, you have made a contribution to the health of the community, to the building up of more sales of milk and, through more uniform and higher quality milk to better prices for this important food.

TWIN CITY MILK PRODUCERS ASSOCIATION

W. A. Moscrip
PRESIDENT

November 25, 1944

QUALITY CONTROL COMMITTEE

Robert Geiger
AGENT

Twin City Milk Producers Association's Award of Merit certificate to Richard for a perfect sanitation record, 1944.

Milk Award of Merit Pins for 1944 (left) and 1947 (right).

The cows stayed in the lower level of the barn—an area we called the cow barn—with access to the cow yard outside. When in the barn, stanchions separated them and secured them from moving around. They had a trough in front of them for hay and silage and a gutter behind for their manure. In the winter, if not too cold, they wandered around the cow yard during the day but always went inside the barn for the night. In the spring, summer, and early autumn, they spent the night in a fenced-in night pasture up a hill, about a five-to-ten-minute walk from the barn. During the day, they roamed over some 20 acres or so of fenced-in land we called the cow pasture, where they ate grass.

Before the girls were born and, later, when they were old enough to stay alone in the house, I was the one to get the cows in the morning from the night pasture. Both Dick and I got up at 5:00 a.m. I called for our dog Sheppy. We had several dogs over the years and named them all Sheppy. Our dogs never stayed in the house but had a doghouse outside or could stay in the barn. Sheppy and I would go through the cow yard and up a hill to the night pasture where we'd go through the gate and round up the cows. They usually came willingly, and Sheppy would go after any stragglers. Ready to be milked, they headed for the barn where Dick waited to put them in their stalls and do the milking.

When we had a hired man in the summer, it was his job to get the cows. One morning there was a thunderstorm with some lightning but no rain. Because of the storm, he refused to go for the cows. He said, "If the boss doesn't go, then I don't." Well, it was left

Cow yard gate leading to pasture on Holasek farm, 1950s.

up to me, so I grabbed an umbrella, called Sheppy, and off we went. By the time I got to the night pasture and got the cows headed toward the barn, the lightning had increased to the point of frightening the cows. They all tried to get through the gate into the cow yard at once, eager to get into the barn. I saw the lightning strike the iron pickets on the fence as the cows went through, and I was carrying an umbrella with a metal core. Finally, I got back to the house, shaking from a close call. Guess it just wasn't my time to go!

Dick milked the cows in the morning and evening. After the

morning milking, he let the cows out of the barn and into the cow yard. He herded them through the cow yard gate into the day pasture and closed the gate behind them. Right outside the gate, they had a block of salt and a big water tank available all day. They meandered about the pasture grazing on their favorite hillside or wooded area. I always went to get them around 4:30 p.m. for the evening milking. I enjoyed those walks, and often Dorothy or Janet, or both, came with me. I loved watching the trees leaf out, and then turn brilliant colors in the fall. I'd usually find an unusual rock or two which I pocketed to add to my collection. It took about a half hour or so to find the cows and bring them home, unless one of them had a calf during the day. A favorite place for them to hide was in wild, scratchy blackberry bushes at the farthest end of the pasture. After Dick finished milking, we'd go with the wheelbarrow in case the calf wasn't able to walk home and bring it home. Some farmers would leave the cow and calf in the pasture overnight and by morning, the calf would be able to walk home, but Dick liked to have them safely in the barn by nightfall.

We depended on the dairy cows for a living with a bit of money coming from the sale of eggs. We always had 50 to 75 chickens and sold eggs to my sister's family, other relatives, and neighbors. I'd also butcher a chicken at least a couple times a month and have either fried or baked chicken for Sunday dinner. We lived frugally, buying only essentials. I had a large vegetable garden and canned over 100 jars of fruits and vegetables each year until we bought a freezer in 1948 when I switched to freezing vegetables. We butchered a cow and pig almost every year which provided our meat and of course we always had milk and eggs. I sewed many of the girls' clothes and kept Dick's overalls and socks mended. When the girls' tennis shoes got too small, Dick would cut out the toe part with a razor so they could continue wearing them around the house, but not to school. Janet was allergic to wool, so I made most of her blouses and corduroy slacks. I can still remember when the first artificial fabric came out in sweaters, and she could finally wear a sweater. It was a yellow nylon cardigan.

Looking at our tax returns indicates how minimal our income was and how detailed we kept records of our farm income and expenses. We did not file income tax before 1941 due to insufficient income. When we did file in 1941, we still had insufficient income to owe tax.

Author's Notes

My parents saved their income tax returns starting with the calendar year 1941. Here is an example of their farm income, expenses, and profit.

FARM INCOME (1941)

Milk	$2,302.52
Eggs	$29.60
Cows	$30.00
Total Income	**$2,362.12**

EXPENSES (1941)

Hired Help	$339.00
Electricity	$117.19
Seed/Plants	$35.60
Grinding Feed	$38.50
Fuel for Farm Work	$16.00
MN State Taxes	$156.65
Insurance	$40.00
Interest on Farm Note	$320.00
Vet Meds	$7.00
Building Repairs	$134.02
Building Fees	$6.00
Truck License	$24.00
Total Expenses	**$1,233.96**

PROFIT (1941)

Net Income	**$1,128.16**

In 1942, my parents began paying income tax. In looking at the returns, 1947 offers an example of a typical year of income and expenses and also provides a list of big-ticket purchases and the annual depreciation allowed for each item. When they bought items like a tractor or milk cooler, they paid the purchase price immediately, but the tax deduction (depreciation) for the item was spread over several years. The annual depreciation for each item was listed with the year's expenses. For example, the tractor purchased in

1946 for $1378.71 was given a life expectancy of ten years. So for the next ten years, they could claim a deduction of $137.87. Here are the items from their 1947 tax return and the depreciation amounts.

ITEMS PURCHASED (1947)

Item	Purchase Date	Life Expectancy	Cost	Depreciation Allowed
Disc	1947 Jan	10 years	$181.00	$18.10
Milk Cooler	1946 Apr	10 years	$347.00	$34.70
Tractor/Plows	1946 Sep	10 years	$1,378.71	$137.87
Horse	1946 Feb	5 years	$85.00	$17.00
Two Horses	1942 Jun	10 years	$80.00	$8.00
Harness	1942 Sep	7 years	$66.00	$9.43
Barn	unknown	25 years	$4,400.00	$176.00
Granary	1924	25 years	$600.00	$24.00
Silo	1938	25 years	$600.00	$24.00

FARM INCOME (1947)

Milk	$4293.97
Eggs	$30.00
Cows	$295.00
Milk Coop Dividends	$8.80
Total Income	**$4,627.77**

EXPENSES (1947)

Farm	$959.57
Depreciation	$449.10
Total Expenses	**$1,408.67**

PROFIT (1947)

Net Income	**$3,219.10**

TAXES PAID (1947)

Income Tax	$203.44
Real Estate Tax	$240.46
Personal Property Tax	$53.90
Total Taxes Paid	**$497.80**

Income in the 1940s was minimal, but they produced much of their own food and lived frugally. Nonetheless, new problems made life as dairy farmers untenable. In 1951, they had to have a well repaired so the cows would continue to have adequate drinking water. It cost $325. This led to other well issues and by 1954, they had issues with the well which might have soon violated the rules regarding milk production. The bulk-milk tank system also came then which drove small farmers out of business, because to survive with the new technology, one had to have at least 40 dairy cows. The new technology made milk production more hygienic, and the farmer no longer had to lift the heavy cans out of the water tank. But it added to the isolation of the farmer, as the milkman no longer came to pick up the cans and visit with the farmer about the weather and crops.

So in the early 1950s, my parents made the difficult decision to convert the barn from dairy cows to raising chickens, in addition to increasing their raspberry and strawberry patches. As a family, we could handle most of the berry picking and marketing of eggs. My parents put an ad in the paper to sell the cows. A few people came and offered to buy one or two, but they had hoped to sell the whole herd. Fortunately, a man came who was looking for a small herd to start his own dairy business. He bought the 16 cows, 2 heifers, and all the milk equipment on May 28, 1954, for $3,140.

Chapter 15 will cover the transition from dairy income to poultry and berry income.

PART III:
JANET HOLASEK WORRALL'S RECOLLECTIONS

11. OBSERVATIONS ON DAILY LIFE

In reminiscing, Dorothy and I always felt fortunate to have grown up on a farm. While we helped with farm chores, our parents never pushed us beyond our limits. While some girls on farms drove the tractor and worked in the field, that was not part of our everyday experience. We enjoyed helping in the garden and learning how vegetables grew and eventually made it to the table. We lived around animals and learned to be cautious but not afraid of them. Some of our neighbors were Czech farmers, but others had city jobs. Had we been boys, I doubt we would have stayed on the farm, as we lived at a transitional time for the family farm.

Mornings began very early with Mother and Daddy getting up around 5:00 a.m. Mother walked up the hill to the night pasture with Sheppy to bring the cows down for milking. Usually, they were waiting by the gate to come out for milking and would head for the barn. Mother closed the gate behind them and followed down the hill. Once Mother brought the cows into the cow yard, Daddy would bring them into the barn to be milked. When finished, he let them out into the big pasture to graze until it was time for the evening milking. Sheppy would come to the house to be fed, and then wander around outside until it was time to get the cows in the late afternoon.

As mentioned earlier, we named all our dogs Sheppy, but Mother had a favorite dog years ago. One day, it wandered down to the main road, got hit by a car, and died. Mother mourned the loss and blamed the purple dress she was wearing for its death. She refused to wear purple after that, claiming it brought bad luck. As a result, I have an aversion to purple and never wear it either, but I tell my kids that the superstition ended with me and that they should feel free to wear purple!

The practice of my parents never allowing their dogs in the house caused a problem years later. Once, my husband Art and I visited my parents, bringing along our Husky Misha, who was a house dog. When we brought him into the house, Daddy was aghast that such an animal was in the house and refused to let poor Misha stay inside. We had to tie him up to a tree outside for the night. The poor dog got fleas and ticks. We had to shorten our stay and of course never brought our dog again on trips to Minnesota.

Returning to our story on the farm, once Daddy had everything ready for the milkman's pickup, he came into the house for breakfast about 7:00 a.m. First, he washed up at the kitchen sink, the only sink on the ground floor. This posed a challenge for Mother, as she often needed water from the sink while cooking. Breakfast was a big meal: bacon/ham and eggs, hot oatmeal, and always coffee. We ate around the kitchen table and often listened to the news on the radio, either WCCO or KSTP. On days when Dorothy and I went to school, Mother ate breakfast quickly in order to make our lunches and help us get ready.

Year round, Daddy had barnyard chores, throwing hay down for the cows and getting silage for them to eat, cleaning horse stalls, and what I considered the worst chore, cleaning the cow barn. He would shovel cow manure from the gutters and toss it into a half-cylinder tank, which ran on a track behind the cows. He pushed the tank out into the barnyard and tipped it over onto the manure pile. Later he shoveled it into a manure spreader pulled by horses or a tractor to distribute in the fields as fertilizer.

Daddy bought his first tractor in 1946, a Ford tractor and plow, for $1,378.71. He had to wait until after World War II when tractors became more available. I'll never forget when he came home with it, and we heard him driving around the corner of the house and Mother said, "There goes the end of our peace and quiet!" But it made many of the farm chores much easier. Daddy still kept the horses for probably ten more years. The tractor was too big to use to plow or cultivate between the rows of raspberries or in the garden. That had to be done with just one horse pulling the plow. Eventually, Daddy bought a smaller tractor, and that meant the end of our having work horses.

Richard resting with Sheppy, work horse and tractor in back, 1950s.

Another chore was splitting and piling wood. We had a wood-burning furnace and stove for many years, and Daddy would go into wooded areas of the cow pasture and "make wood," as we called it, for our fuel supply. He usually took the pickup truck and loaded the wood in the back. He had no power tools but used a variety of saws and an axe. Trees had sometimes fallen naturally, and he would saw them into pieces that fit in the back of the truck to bring closer to the house. There, he split them into smaller pieces for the kitchen stove and left some in big pieces for the furnace. He would throw the pieces on a heap, and both he and Mother would stack the wood into piles. I remember helping with this often and never appreciated the mice and snakes that made their homes under the wood. We had three big wood piles; one right outside the cow yard, one down by the garden fence, and one in the cow pasture. In the fall, Daddy would load wood from the wood piles into the truck, bring it to the house, and throw it into the basement through an open window. We would stack it again in the basement next to the furnace and wood box, which could be cranked up to the kitchen pantry near the wood stove.

Mention of the woodpile always brought back one of Mother's worst nightmares. It happened when I was about two years old and was going to go with Daddy to shut one of the gates. Dorothy sat in the kitchen with her coloring book while Mother finished the supper dishes. After cleaning up, she went outside and asked Daddy where I was, and he said that he had no idea. They frantically began to search the house, and then the yard, trying to find me as it was getting dark. Finally, Mother started running to the neighbors to use their phone to call the police. She slipped on the damp grass falling flat on her back, but picked herself up and ran toward the garden which was the shortcut to the neighbors. As she approached the garden, she turned slightly to the left and saw my hair and part of my face. I was sitting at the end of the nearby woodpile, crying. She ran over, picked me up, hugged me, and wept with joy. After that, Mother always knew where Dorothy and I were at dusk. Even in her nineties, she said she would have nightmares that I had disappeared.

By November of each year, the folks had to put up the snow fence. They stretched it parallel to the road coming up to the house and along the road that encircled the house. This prevented drifts from developing on the driveway. In the spring, they rolled the snow fence up and stored it until the next winter.

Our land had a lot of rocks which had to be removed before the fields could be planted. Daddy fastened together several pieces of wood into something of a platform that we called a stone boat. He would hitch the horses or tractor up to it, and head out to the field to remove all sizes of stones from the field. Some were huge! He took them to a couple places on the farm near a ravine and rolled them down unto what we called the stone pile.

Despite this strenuous work, Daddy never complained of any physical problems. He did, however, go to a chiropractor for several years for back treatments which helped him keep in shape. Given the frequency of farm accidents, he never lost a finger or suffered any injuries from machinery. He did take Nutrilite vitamin and mineral pills regularly, being convinced of their value by a salesperson

Aerial view of Holasek farm after snow storm: Richard plowing road around house with wooden V-shaped snowplow pulled by two horses (center bottom); house, barn with track for manure carrier, silo, corn crib, wood pile covered with snow (center left). Image from Minneapolis Star-Journal, *March 15, 1940. Copyright Star Tribune Media Company LLC. Used with permission.*

named Marie. She came every month with a fresh supply of pills. Maybe they helped keep him healthy, because he never suffered anything but the common cold and headaches until his later years.

For as long as I can remember, we had only one family doctor. Dr. Frank J. Kucera had an office on Excelsior Boulevard for the entire 55 years he remained in practice. He delivered both Dorothy and me, and we went to him regularly for vaccinations, checkups, sore throats, and whatever ailments we had. Mother trusted him implicitly, and he continued to be her doctor until his retirement in 1976. I can still visualize going into his reception room with Mother and glancing at the other patients waiting their turn. Dr. Kucera's nurse managed appointments and collected payments in her adjoining office. Always wearing a crisp white uniform, she was a friendly but no-nonsense woman. Dr. Kucera's office had an examination table, chair, cabinets, and a rolltop desk where he sat to write prescriptions. A medicinal smell permeated the room. Dr. Kucera wore a white coat and glasses, had a slight mustache, and conveyed a kind, gentle manner.

He would make house calls and see patients at his house after office hours. When I was about six years old, Dorothy and I were playing outside. I found a pretty stone about three inches in diameter and wondered how high I could throw it. So up it went and came down on my head! Blood spurted from the wound. Mother wrapped my head in a towel, Daddy came running, and we all jumped in the car and headed for Dr. Kucera's home, as it was after office hours. Dr. Kucera in his calm manner examined and cleaned the wound. I don't

Portrait of Dr. Frank Kucera, oil on jute canvas painted by Milli Oden, 1972. Courtesy of the Hopkins Historical Society (HHS1950.24).

remember how he treated it, but he assured my parents that it was not serious, to treat the area gently, and it would heal in a few weeks.

A well-known member of the Czech community, Dr. Kucera contributed much to the town of Hopkins. He served on the school board for 27 years, was a member and officer in Sokol for many years, a charter member of the Czech Fraternal Life Association (ZCBJ), an avid supporter of Raspberry Day, and involved in many other Hopkins activities. He was named "Czech of the Year" by the Czechoslovakian Heritage Festival in 1976. As city health officer for Hopkins, he led the effort to give the Salk anti-polio vaccine to school children in April 1955.

Hopkins Raspberry Festival Royalty with Dr. Frank Kucera (center back), 1980. Courtesy of the Hopkins Historical Society.

His parents had come to the United States as children during the Czech immigrant wave of the 1860s and 1870s. With other Czechs, they settled on farmland in southern Minnesota. Frank was one of 13 children. He graduated from Hutchinson High School in 1913, entered the University of Minnesota in 1915, and graduated from the University's medical school in 1921. Frank met his wife Alma Foss when she was a nurse at Asbury Hospital in Minneapolis. They married in 1921 when Dr. Kucera started his practice in Hopkins in family medicine, continuing there until his retirement in December 1976 at the age of 82. Our family always felt a close bond to him because of our common Czech heritage.

Funerals and paying respect to families who lost loved ones was very important to my parents and the Czech community. As a child, I remember my parents dressing up in the evening to visit relatives of a deceased member of our community. Daddy would change his overalls and wear dress pants and a nice shirt, while Mother wore her black, accordion-pleated skirt with a blouse. We would all get into the car and drive to the Strobeck Funeral Home in Hopkins, which was the funeral home that everyone seemed to use. An open casket was the practice then, and visitors gathered around to comment on what a good person the deceased had been and how nice he or she looked. We stayed for about half an hour, talking with relatives, giving our condolences, and ending with hugs and words of sympathy, promising to be at the funeral.

Mother and Daddy also paid regular visits to the Shady Oak Lake Cemetery where our relatives along with many other Czechs were buried. I remember walking up the steps of the cemetery as Daddy lifted the latch to open the gate. Beautiful pine trees provided shade in many areas. My parents brought flowers to plant, especially on Memorial Day. Pansies and geraniums were favorites. This was an important time of remembrance for my parents, as they paid tribute to their parents and others in the family. Daddy would always shake his head as he looked at his brother Lilliard's grave, and Mother would stand by her parents' grave with tears in her eyes, whispering how she missed them. Then we all soberly walked around looking at gravestones and reminiscing. Many Czechs were also buried in a nearby Catholic cemetery and in the cemetery adjacent to the John Hus Presbyterian Church, now Faith Presbyterian Church.

We did have one annual event we looked forward to, and that was the Raspberry Parade and Festival. However, picking our own raspberries sometimes kept us from going, as did the years when we feared getting polio in a crowd. When we did go, all of us dressed in our best clothes. Daddy wore his only suit, a blue woolen one. How he survived the heat in that woolen suit, I will never know! We always stood in the same place, in a shaded area near the end of the parade route. There, we watched the floats, applauded when the Raspberry Queen went by, and cheered for the bands and baton twirlers. When the parade finished, everyone went to the sunny fairgrounds where the kids enjoyed carnival rides and the farmers gathered to discuss what they usually talked about: the weather and how it was affecting the crops. We would stay until about 4:30 p.m.

Shady Oak Lake Cemetery.

Holasek gravesite: John (father), Mary (mother), Lilliard, Richard, Evelyn, and Dorothy, 2022.

Joseph (1826-1890) and Marie (1832-1912) Holasek's gravestone with Joseph's inscription (front) and Marie's inscription (side).

Joseph's inscription (left): "I am waiting for you in this dark tomb my wife so that you can take a rest here after all your work. You my dear children look at our tomb, it will be your home in this dark valley." Marie's inscription (right): "My dear husband, I am coming to you after my work so that I can rest by your side in this common dark tomb." Translation by Petr Kohout.

Evelyn's parents Petrolina (1878-1939) and Stanley (1878-1949) Svec.

at the latest, and then had to head home to milk the cows.

We never knew what a vacation was; there was always work waiting to be done, especially in the summers. I remember returning to school in the fall and, on the first day back, the teacher would go around the room and ask how we spent our summer. Many students talked about trips and vacations they had taken, and I was always embarrassed because I had nothing to say. Some families also went to sporting events, but Daddy could never understand people "wasting" their time on such things when they could be working!

We never spent money on frivolous things, but never worried about having money for the necessities of food and clothing. My parents paid all bills with cash, and they never had a credit card or checking account until the 1980s. If they needed a check, they would get a money order at the bank. For several years, banks gave gifts for deposits, and we acquired many blankets, dishes, lamps, and saucepans this way. Mother always kept a close watch on which banks had offers, and money would be deposited there to take advantage of those offers. For a time, grocery stores gave green and gold stamps with every purchase. Mother collected these and in the evenings, we glued them into the stamp books. Once filled, we enjoyed looking in the catalog of gifts to see what we should get. Eventually, the stores stopped giving stamps which was a great disappointment.

Daddy always wore overalls and a blue shirt underneath—long-sleeved in the winter and short-sleeved in the summer. His shoes seemed heavy to me, brown ankle-high work shoes with laces, worn with brown and white work socks. On occasion, when he went to the

Richard's ashtray, wallet, Association stamp, eyeglasses and watch, which he always kept tied on a shoestring in his overalls' front pocket.

grocery store, he wore khaki pants and his blue shirt. He did have his one good suit, white shirts, and dress shoes for weddings and funerals.

Daddy was never overweight, even though he ate meat three times a day as well as Mother's homemade bread and pies. We always had dessert, especially after the evening meal. He needed all the calories he could get given how hard he worked every day. He could tolerate pain well and despite having considerable dental work, bridges and fillings, he refused to have novocaine, hating the feeling of numbness afterwards. I'll never know how he endured the pain.

He also suffered from what I now recognize as migraines. I would see him sitting at the kitchen table with his head in his hands, glasses set aside. Once I asked him if he had taken aspirins, and he said, "I grind them up and eat them like cereal." I didn't know about migraines then, but it is clear that he suffered from them, and I have inherited them! Mother, however, never had a headache and one time asked me, "What does it feel like when your head hurts?"

While Mother had a driver's license and kept it renewed as long as she lived (99 years), Daddy always did the driving. I think in the distant past, she had had a bad scare and never drove again. So Daddy did all the driving for groceries, doctor and dentist appointments, and our school events. He somehow managed it along with the farm work. We made it to all our major school activities including basketball games, which was remarkable. The first car I remember was a 1940 grey Nash, later replaced with a green Chevrolet in 1953. That's the car Dorothy and I learned to drive in and the last car I remember before leaving home in 1960. It had an automatic shift, and I suspect Daddy thought it a necessity in teaching us to drive.

Once, when I went to Hopkins with Daddy on a trip to the hardware store, I asked if I could get an ice cream cone. He was in a hurry and said, "No, there isn't time today." Later he said how badly he felt saying no, and whenever we went out again, he always asked if I wanted ice cream, trying to make up for his earlier denial.

There was never any question that Dorothy and I were dearly loved by our parents. They never got angry with us. The one exception was when Dorothy was working in a law office and bought a record player. Her boss Mr. Vennum gave her a ride home with it. She put it in the living room, and Daddy was furious with such an unnecessary purchase. He actually did not talk to her for three days!

I always wondered if Mother ever regretted leaving Hopkins

and her secretarial job for the much harder life as a farmer's wife. When I asked her, she always said, "But then I wouldn't have had you and Dorothy." Subject ended.

Mother had her outside chores including taking care of the chickens. Even though we had only 50 or 75 chickens most of the time, she had to keep their feeders and water jars full and gather eggs. She still had to shell corn for them using the hand sheller, and then brought the corncobs to the kitchen to start a fire in the wood stove. Once the weather warmed in the spring, the berries needed hoeing and garden planting began. Mother did most of this after Daddy plowed the garden area. He then went to plant corn, oats, and other crops. Mother kept busy helping outside as well as tending the house. In the winter, she sewed a lot, making sunbonnets, all her everyday dresses, and many of our clothes. She always wore a dress, not starting to wear pants until the 1970s.

We called our noon meal between 12:00 and 1:00 p.m. dinner. It was always a big meal of meat, potatoes, a vegetable, bread or *kolach*, and dessert—usually a blueberry or apple pie or cake. Once finished, it was back to work. We never took naps.

Mother baked two pies every week (usually blueberry), wonderful rye bread, and a braided bread called *houska*. In addition, her oatmeal and chocolate chip cookies always filled the cookie jar, and a white or chocolate cake was there for snacking. On days when time permitted, Mother made wonderful pot roasts on top of the stove. First, she browned the meat, and then added water, letting it simmer for a few hours before adding potatoes, onions, and carrots. I often came by and sliced pieces off the roast while it was cooking. Meat seemed to have much more of a natural flavor than meat today. Once the pot roast finished cooking, Mother made a delicious gravy to use on the potatoes. A favorite of ours was the chicken that she made in her cast iron skillet. First, she dipped the chicken pieces in flour, then egg, and then flour again before placing them in the pan. She baked the chicken in the oven, and it came out with a golden brown crispy coating…so very good! While pasta is popular today, we rarely had it, except in a casserole that Mother made with elbow macaroni, hamburger, celery, onions, and tomato juice. She also made wonderful chicken noodle soup with homemade noodles. Another favorite of ours were her plum dumplings. The only prepared foods that we bought were frozen fish sticks and, occasionally, TV dinners. Otherwise, Mother cooked all our meals from scratch.

Famous for her delicious *kolach*, Mother made her own poppy seed and prune filling. She grew poppy seed in her garden, and I can still visualize the pods among the vegetables. Once she extracted the poppy seed from the pods, she ground it in a hand-grinding machine. The ground poppy seed fell into a little drawer at the bottom of the machine. She mixed it with other ingredients, and it was ready for use. For the prune filling, she boiled the prunes, then pitted and mashed them, adding several spices to make the most delicious filling. She made her own dough, and I still have the huge bowl she used. I can still see her punching down the dough once it had risen. She put the dough on her wooden board and with a spoon divided it into small pieces which she patted and stretched into four-inch circles. In the middle of each, she put a spoonful of either prune or poppy seed filling, and pulled and attached the left and right sides together, followed by the other two sides, making a square *kolach*. She placed them side by side on a baking sheet and brushed the tops with butter using her *stetka* made from chicken feathers. They sat for a half hour to rise and baked for 35 minutes. When done, she masterfully got them out of the pan with one quick shake. She brushed the tops with more butter and let them cool. For the next several days, we all enjoyed eating her *kolach*, but Mother said the only time she really liked them was sitting down with a cup of coffee and a couple *kolaches* when they were still warm!

At some point in the afternoon, if time permitted, Mother went down to get the mail and paper. We had a mailbox at the end of the driveway and a newspaper box across the road. As long as I can remember, we got a daily newspaper, *The Minneapolis Tribune*. I have vivid memories of Mother bringing the paper into the house and immediately opening it on the kitchen table to the comics page. It was one of her few moments of total escapism as she read her favorite columns: Mary Worth, Little Orphan Annie, Dick Tracy, and Rex Morgan. I could just see her momentarily enter their worlds before having to return to the reality of getting the cows or starting dinner.

Mother kept an immaculate house and saw it as a reflection of her as a housekeeper. After visiting a cousin, Mother remarked on what a good housekeeper the cousin was because "there was not

Observations on Daily Life | 141

Bowl Evelyn used to make kolach *and bread dough.*

Evelyn's poppy seed grinder.

Household items: iron, tea kettle, tins for marshmallows and cinnamon.

Coffee cup from Bohemia with inscription: "God I love coffee."

a speck of dust left anywhere in her house!" Mother did a regular spring and fall housecleaning when she washed all the windows, curtains, and cleaned out closets. She would store or air winter blankets, coats, and other winter clothing to make the seasonal shift. Dorothy and I helped with this as much as possible.

We also had our regular chores. We took turns every week setting the table and helping with the meals and dishes afterwards. On Saturdays, we had specific chores; one of us would use a dust mop on the wooden floors and wet mop the wooden steps leading upstairs. We had a bucket of water and an old cloth, probably a worn-out washcloth or piece of an old towel. The other one would dust furniture and vacuum as well as clean the sink and toilet. Every week, we got an allowance for these chores. At first, it was $0.25, and then in 1952, I remember Daddy was so happy Eisenhower won the presidency that he celebrated by raising our allowance to $0.50! He always paid us on Friday.

About 4:30 p.m. every day, Mother and Sheppy would go for the cows. Sometimes, Dorothy and I went with her. Mother had a great appreciation for nature which Dorothy and I inherited. She loved different kinds of trees: oak, maple, birch, and elm. A rock or two always caught her eye, and I still have the special tray that Daddy made for her collection with several of her prized stones.

The cows would usually be off some distance, grazing in the pasture. It took about half an hour to bring them home, and then Daddy let them into the barn for milking. When he finished, he took them up to the night pasture. Sometimes, Dorothy and I went with him.

Tray made by Richard filled with Evelyn's prized stones.

At about 6:30 p.m., he would come in, wash up at the kitchen sink, and we would have supper at the round table in the dining room. Again, we had a big meal with meat, usually fried potatoes, vegetables, bread, and dessert. In the 1950s, Mother bought a deep fat fryer in which she made marvelous fried chicken and corn fritters. These became a favorite for all of us.

After the dishes were washed and put away, we watched our favorite television programs. Our first television, purchased in December 1950, was a small black-and-white Philco, which we put in the corner of the living room. It sat on a turntable so we could watch it in either the dining or living room. Everyone enjoyed shows like *Red Skelton*, *What's My Line* with Bennett Cerf and Dorothy Kilgallen, the *$64,000 Question* (especially when Joyce Brothers was on), *Ed Sullivan*, *I Love Lucy*, *Milton Berle*, *Jackie Gleason/the Honeymooners* and *This is Your Life*. Dorothy and I had favorites on Saturday morning like *The Lone Ranger* and *Cisco Kid*. Dorothy would have periods of intense admiration for certain shows like the

Perry Como Show and for certain Hollywood stars like June Allyson. We never missed the Miss America contest with another of Dorothy's favorites, MC Bert Parks. Our television time was restricted to a couple of hours per week, and this was contingent on keeping our grades up in school. However, if I watched *The Lone Ranger* as part of my two hours, Dorothy could also watch it without it counting toward her two hours. As you can imagine, this took some careful planning on the part of both of us to maximize our television viewing!

The television brought relief from the daily routine of work for all of us, but especially for our parents. They had little opportunity for entertainment and laughter, and this brought us together. We often took a break and made popcorn in a wire basket over the stove or enjoyed Mother's blueberry pie. I remember evenings sitting together with eyes focused on the little box in the corner as among our happiest times.

12. VEGETABLE GARDEN

Mother always had a large vegetable garden which supplied us with fresh vegetables in the summer and canned or frozen produce in the winter. The garden area was to the north of the house, down a slight hill, and just outside the iron fence which encircled the house and barn. Every spring Daddy plowed the garden area, and together they marked straight rows with twine stretched the length of the row. Then Mother took over the planting.

A bit to the east of this main garden, she had a "hotbed" which was a wooden frame set in the ground with glass windows over it where she started early plants. Alongside the "hotbed" was her asparagus bed and next to it four or five rhubarb plants. During the spring she would don her sunbonnet, take what she called her utility pan—her precious stainless steel pan purchased at Dayton's on sale—along with a sharp paring knife, and head for the asparagus bed. She would cut the asparagus plants right below ground level, fill her pan, and head back to the house to make supper. We had asparagus all spring, but there was never enough to freeze. I remember its wonderful flavor, unlike the rather tasteless commercial asparagus found in today's supermarkets.

The main garden had a few rows of strawberries, raspberries, or blackberries, and alternating rows of lettuce, spinach, carrots, green and yellow string beans, peas, radishes, onions, green peppers, tomatoes, cucumbers (picklers and larger ones for table consumption),

One of Evelyn's many sunbonnets. She never left the house without one, which contributed to her beautiful complexion throughout her life.

melons, cabbage, kohlrabi, corn, and squash. All summer long, we had fresh lettuce, radishes, cucumbers, and other vegetables with every meal. Radishes, small green onions, and lettuce usually came first while the cucumbers, beans, peas, and other vegetables matured a bit later.

The garden required attention all summer, mainly to keep the weeds out and the soil loose. Some of the rows were wide enough apart for Daddy to cultivate between them with one horse. After Daddy cultivated, Mother hoed around each plant or along the sides of a row of string beans. She had her own special hoe which Daddy kept sharpened. Many of the vegetables like lettuce and beans required thinning once they were an inch or so high. Mother never used the popular metal cages for tomatoes but pounded wooden stakes by each plant and tied the vines up with strips of cloth from old sheets. Vegetables required several pickings. I remember straddling the rows of green and yellow string beans, picking only those of the right length. If I missed some, they would be too big and tough by the next picking. We anxiously awaited the first cucumbers, which Mother sliced and salted with onions for supper. A couple of weeks after the first cucumbers, there would be enough to make a batch of pickles, which made for late nights, especially during berry season.

Before we purchased the freezer, Mother canned vegetables, plums, peaches, pears, and other fruits in glass jars. She made applesauce with apples from the tree in our woods and canned plums from trees in front of the house for her famous plum dumplings. I remember her sterilizing the glass jars and lids, filling them, and gingerly placing them in the large canning kettle of boiling water on top of the stove. She carefully removed them after the requisite cooking time, being sure no doors or windows were open to cause a draft that would crack the hot jars. Once cooled, she took the jars to the basement, placing them on shelves in what we called the vegetable room. The freezer greatly eased the process of preserving, as many fruits and vegetables could be frozen rather than preserved in glass jars. She froze raspberries and strawberries and when blueberries went on sale in the summer, she would freeze at least seven crates (84 boxes) for her famous blueberry pies. In the winter, she baked two pies every week which Daddy had no trouble consuming!

Evelyn's fruit jars used in canning.

Dorothy and I helped with the picking and preparing of vegetables for freezing. Green and yellow string beans had to be tipped and cut. Peas had to be shelled, which seemed like an endless job given the small amount of the final product. In the evening, we would sit on the back porch where it was cool and spend hours opening the pods and stripping the peas from the pods leaving us with sore fingers.

Mother grew several kinds of tomatoes. Some we ate fresh all summer long and others she canned for stewed tomatoes in the winter. A favorite of mine were the little yellow tomatoes shaped like a gourd, which Mother put in our lunches in the fall. She also made pickles, both bread and butter and dill. I remember helping stuff the branches of dill into the jars with the cucumbers before the sealing process. While the freezer was a great help in preserving vegetables like green beans and corn, other vegetables like tomatoes, cucumbers (pickles), and red beets, as well as peaches, and pears, still required canning using glass jars and the hot water bath.

Another favorite of ours was corn on the cob which came mid to late summer. Daddy and I would have contests to see who could eat the most; we usually stopped at five ears each. Raccoons often got the first ears and remained a constant problem throughout the summer, thus the need for scarecrows and small windmills on poles in the corn patch. Then there was the problem of smut, a fungus that grew on some of the ears which we had to discard. There is an old story that the number of rows on an ear of corn is always even. At one time, a prize was offered to whomever could grow an ear of corn with an uneven number of rows. Certain to win, a nearby farmer cut one row out on several ears of corn early in the growing season, but it did not work. It was apparent that the ears had been tampered with and a scar remained in the place of the eliminated row.

Freezing corn took an assembly-line approach. First, the corn had to be picked and husked. We husked the corn over a big bucket outside. Inside, Dorothy and I put together the waxed, cardboard boxes, and inserted the plastic bag liner. Mother did the blanching of the corn in the big kettle on the stove, and then placed the corn in ice-cold water. She stood each cooled ear on end in her special wooden bowl and with a sharp knife cut down the side of the ear, rotating it until all the corn was off. Once the bowl was three-quarters full, she scooped the corn kernels into the plastic bag, the top held open with a funnel, while Dorothy or I held the box steady. Once full, the top of the plastic bag was twisted and secured with a tie, the box was closed and ready for the freezer. We froze at least 40 quarts of corn every summer.

Mother had a fondness for the banana muskmelon, a yellow-green melon about 8-to-12-inches long. I remember going down to the garden with her, finding a ripe one, sitting on a nearby stump, and with a knife she conveniently had with her, she would slit it lengthwise and scrape out the seeds. With spoons suddenly appearing out of her pocket, we would sit and eat the whole thing. At one time the melons grew in such excess that Daddy took 24 to the Highview stand to sell along with some ever-bearing strawberries.

Carrots waited to be harvested until the fall. Mother dug out the carrots with a fork with wide tines, and Dorothy and I shook the dirt off them, pulled off the green tops, and put them in the wagon for the trip up to the house. We liked to watch for double ones or those with an interesting shape. We hauled them to the basement where Mother packed them in sand in a big Red Wing crock in the vegetable room. They stayed surprisingly crisp all winter. We also brought squash, pumpkins, cabbages, and onions home in the wagon for storage in the basement.

Potatoes took a lot of care, starting with the cutting of the seed potatoes—Mother's job—and the planting, which Daddy did with a special hand planter. Once the potato plant came up, hoeing to ward off weeds and to loosen the soil around the plant kept the whole family busy. Dorothy and I hoed side by side and once Dorothy accidentally chopped off the plant at ground level. Worried what Daddy who was hoeing nearby would say, we decided to just stick the cut off plant back in the ground. Within a half hour, the plant had wilted, and when Daddy came by to check on us, he asked, "What happened to this little guy?" It was obvious. I guess he decided it was bound to happen occasionally, so he just rubbed his forehead and told us to be more careful. That remained an oft-told story on the farm, bringing considerable laughter each time we remembered the woe-begone-wilted potato plant in a row of vigorous plants.

In the fall, Daddy dug the potatoes with a special fork, and Mother gathered and put them into a sack. I enjoyed watching this and sometimes helped. It was always a guess as to how many potatoes would be under each plant and how widely spread out they would be. The sacked potatoes went into the vegetable room in the basement and stayed fresh nearly all winter long.

The time also came in the fall to make sauerkraut. Mother hauled the cabbages in the wagon from the garden to the basement cellarway. She peeled off the outside leaves, stacked the heads, and got the area ready. Daddy brought out the special wooden frame with cutting blades and positioned it on top of two sawhorses. A five-gallon Red Wing crock was placed underneath the blades. Mother cut the cabbage heads in half and positioned the cut half over the cutting blades. She and Daddy took turns pushing the cabbage back and forth across the blades to shred it. They paused occasionally to add caraway seed, salt, and other ingredients to the shredded cabbage. When the crock was filled, they placed a plate and large rock on top of the shredded cabbage to weigh it down. There it stayed to process and when finished, it was the best sauerkraut ever.

I have never found a store-bought sauerkraut to equal its wonderful flavor and texture. Mother also made sauerkraut in glass jars to supplement what was in the crocks. I have fond memories of eating it right out of the jar when she brought one up for dinner. Czechs loved pork and sauerkraut, a staple for them throughout the cold, Minnesota winters.

Having a garden and preserving large quantities of fruits and vegetables reduced the food we had to purchase in stores and made us somewhat self-sufficient. Eventually, the wooden cabbage shredder outlived its usefulness, so several years ago I donated it to a museum in Wyoming.

One of Evelyn's Red Wing crocks.

13. DOROTHY AND JANET: GROWING UP

Most of my memories of growing up on the farm involve my sister Dorothy, who was three years older than me. Not having neighbors close by, we spent our time together doing household chores, playing with our dolls, playing school, reading, or just hanging out. Playdates didn't exist in our farm culture as they do today. Later, in school, we each had a good friend, but the distance between houses in what was then rural Eden Prairie kept us from frequent visits with friends, so Dorothy and I relied on each other for company. We were best friends and always supportive of each other. There was no rivalry or jealousy between us. We both excelled in school and were the valedictorians of our respective classes. Teachers never treated me as Dorothy's "little sister." We each made our own mark being separated by three years. Plus, we didn't look like each other; Dorothy had blonde hair, blue eyes, and fair skin while I had brown hair, dark brown eyes, and darker skin.

Dorothy was more stubborn and independent than I was. She was more of a leader, perhaps because she was the oldest, while I was more comfortable in a supportive role. Mother used to tell a story that when we were small and one of our aunts visited, Dorothy was asked to recite a poem she had just learned, which she did perfectly. Then I said in a small voice, "I know that too," and to the amazement of everyone I recited it perfectly.

While I hated conflict and tended to be the peacemaker,

Dorothy would hold her ground, unwilling to compromise if she felt she was right. But this did not mean she wasn't a kind, compassionate person. She loved being around people and could be depended on to help anyone in need. She was just not easily swayed to change her viewpoint.

I tended to spend more time in the kitchen than Dorothy did. I enjoyed helping Mother bake or make meals. I would often follow her outside to help hang the freshly washed clothes or just watch her feed the baby chicks or shell corn. I would even help her pile wood into a neat stack once Daddy had split it into small pieces. Mother and I were very close, and we just enjoyed talking with each other.

As a child, Dorothy's stubbornness came out in tantrums. Frustrated, Mother asked Dr. Kucera what she should do. He suggested telling Dorothy that she had to go upstairs and stay there alone until she was done with her tantrum. So when Dorothy had her next tantrum, Mother gently took her by the hand and as they headed upstairs, Mother explained that Dorothy had to stay there until she calmed down. Halfway up the stairs, Dorothy's tantrum stopped, and that was the end of them!

Mother recalls that occasionally, Dorothy could be shy and that she was very nervous on her first day of school, not knowing anyone. Mother told her to remember that other little girls would also be afraid, and that Dorothy should help them by going up to them and making friends. Not surprisingly, Dorothy came home that first day talking nonstop about her new friend, Mary Ann. I never experienced that apprehension because when I started school, Dorothy was there to sit with me on the bus and take me to the first-grade classroom where the teacher made all the new students feel welcome.

Mother tried to give us as many new experiences as possible. On one trip I will never forget, we went to see the Ringling Bros. and Barnum & Bailey Circus. Even though this was when Dorothy and I were quite young, Mother arranged for us to see it, taking us on the bus to Minneapolis. We sat very high in the auditorium but could still see all three rings going on simultaneously: the trapeze artists, elephants parading around, and clowns juggling bowling pins. I think Mother enjoyed it as much if not more than we did, as she had limited opportunities to get out.

Even before we went to school, Dorothy and I liked to "play school." We had small school desks and chairs in the kitchen where Mother spent most of her time. Because the kitchen had a wood stove for cooking, it was the warmest room in the house. In our desks we had paper, pencils, coloring books, and crayons. Mother enjoyed our company and always showed interest in our work. I remember my desk sat right in front of the kitchen window facing south. In the winter it caught the warm sun. We spent hours playing there with Mother offering suggestions of things to draw and color. Sometimes, we even brought our dolls and doll beds and set them beside our desks.

In the summer, we put our dolls in their strollers and pushed them on the road around our house. In the late 1940s and early 1950s when polio was a threat, our parents would not let us go to any places with a crowd. That meant we could not go to the annual Raspberry Festival and Parade in Hopkins. So Dorothy and I had our

Janet's desk and chair with her favorite doll.

own parade! With Daddy and Mother sitting on the swing by the road which circled our house, we pushed our doll carriages and pulled a wagon past them to their applause.

Mother had a fear of flies, which I now realize coincided with the polio scare. She would never eat anything that a fly sat on, and she always had a fly swatter handy. As I look back, it was common knowledge then that flies could get the polio germ from sitting on feces, garbage, or unsanitary surfaces and carry it to food left out in the open. People eating this food could catch polio. When the Salk polio vaccine came out in 1955, she made sure Dorothy and I were in line to be vaccinated. We had all seen too many cases of polio victims in iron lungs or disabled in some way and considered ourselves very fortunate to be among the first to get the vaccine.

Starting in about the 1950s, Mother took Dorothy and me to Minneapolis nearly every Saturday, necessitated by my health issues. My parents thought Dr. Oscar Lindquist, a chiropractor recommended by a friend, might help me. He had an office on Nicollet Avenue in Minneapolis. Mother took this opportunity to enroll Dorothy and me in gymnastics, tap dance, and baton twirling classes in nearby studios. These classes continued on Saturdays for three or four years, giving us the opportunity to mingle with other children and perform.

On these trips, Mother taught us how to cross streets in her own unique way. She always looked at the light for oncoming traffic and when the light turned red and traffic stopped, she would say, "It's red now so we can cross!" She didn't watch for the pedestrians' green light but rather the vehicles' red light, which meant "go" for her.

Fortunately, a bus that went into Minneapolis had a regular schedule from the Glen Lake Sanatorium which was just a mile from our house. We could walk there, or Daddy drove us to catch the bus. Since the bus route started at the sanatorium, we had our pick of seats and had our favorites. We loved the bus ride. It took about 45 minutes going through Glen Lake, down Excelsior Boulevard, through St. Louis Park, by Lake Calhoun, up Lake Street, and eventually into Minneapolis. We would get off on Hennepin Avenue, either at 7th or 8th Street, and walk the block up to Nicollet Avenue, where all the main stores were as well as Dr. Lindquist's office. There were two dime stores on the corners of 7th and Nicollet, Kresge and Woolworth. On the other corners were Dayton's and Donaldson's and down a block or two was Powers. Along the way, we would look in the show window of our favorite shoe store, Chandler's.

These were wonderful Saturday outings for the three of us. We enjoyed shopping, especially the Early Bird sales on Saturdays in Dayton's basement from 9:00 a.m. to noon. I can still picture us racing down the steps to the basement to be among the first shoppers and get the best selection of sale items. We saved so much money by shopping sales, something that has remained with me. If there is a sale, I need to check it out. By 4:00 p.m., we were ready to return home. We would arrange ahead of time, consulting printed schedules, what bus we would catch. Then Daddy would meet us either at the sanatorium or Glen Lake store. In the summer, we walked home. On a hot day, Mother would make sure I walked in her shadow so I wouldn't get overheated.

Once Dorothy and I were older, we went to Minneapolis by ourselves. Dorothy had braces for two years and went to her orthodontist Dr. Colby in the early 1950s. I remember the day they were removed, May 21, 1954. She was so happy, and her teeth looked beautiful. When we went to Minneapolis by ourselves, Dorothy went to Dr. Colby for adjustments on her braces, and I went to Dr. Lindquist. Then we would shop! Before waiting for the bus on Hennepin Avenue, we would buy one of our favorite comic books—*Archie*, *Betty and Veronica*, or *Jughead*—to read on the ride home.

Dorothy and I both loved to read. Once we were in school, we brought home library books and spent hours reading. In the summer, when the school library was not available, Daddy took us every two weeks to the public library in Hopkins to get books. For several summers, we were hooked on the *Nancy Drew* mystery books. The library limited the number of books we could check out, and we quickly read through them, eagerly awaiting our next trip. I still remember the smell of books as we entered the library and can visualize the librarian at the desk. Once we selected our books, the librarian watched as we signed the card for each book. She stamped each card with the due date and filed them in a rectangular wooden box on her desk. She stamped the printed slips—glued to the inside of the books—with the due date. When signing the card, we always looked to see who had checked the book out before us. Today I think of the loss of this personal interaction as I electronically check out books in the library, never having to speak a word to anyone. I believe that we have lost something valuable!

In the 1940s and early 1950s, when women generally stayed home to raise their children, salesmen used to come to the house. The "Watkins man," representing the J. R. Watkins Company, came about once a month selling baking products, soaps, liniment, and household items. My mother welcomed his visits to break the routine of her day, as well as to see what products he had to offer.

One salesman I remember vividly sold encyclopedias. This was long before we could access information on Google. We had to depend on the encyclopedias in school to write our reports. I remember working in the library using the *Encyclopedia Britannica* or *World Book* to write a report and wishing we had a set at home. To my great delight, a salesman came by in the early 1950s selling a 12-volume set on the installment plan. I remember sitting at the dining room table as he displayed the diagrams of the human body, solar system, and maps of the world. I envisioned spending evenings looking at the maps and reading about different countries. Mother and Daddy showed enthusiasm, and the salesman came back three times to try to persuade us to purchase the set. But it was not to be. To my great disappointment, Daddy decided not to buy it because we had access to encyclopedias in school. The salesman left as disappointed as I was, leaving information where he could be reached if Daddy changed his mind.

During the summer, when Dorothy and I were young, we spent as much time as possible playing outside. On the south side of our home, we would play house using old orange crates as our cupboard. Mother would give us old jars and lids to use as dishes. We left them out during the winter and one spring we discovered a snake had curled up inside one of the lids! We also had swings nearby. Daddy made them out of rope with a board seat and hung them on a tree. We spent hours swinging and had contests to see who could swing the highest or jump off the farthest. We would also pick leaves off the locust tree in front of the house and pretend they were money.

Janet and Dorothy on their swing in the winter, c. 1946.

Richard standing on back of truck with Janet and Dorothy standing on truck's running board, c. 1946.

We did cartwheels, back bends, and headstands. We twirled our batons and threw them up to see how high we could toss and still catch them. When our cousins came over, we played with our dolls and when older, played hide-and-seek and kick the can in the yard, and seven-up against the brick house. When Dorothy learned to drive and got her license, we went to play tennis on the courts by the Glen Lake Sanatorium. When finished we would go to the nearby grocery store to get a pint of chocolate ice cream, and ate it in the car with the spoons we had brought from home.

Cousins after practicing baton twirling, left to right: Dorothy, Janet, Pat White, Kay White; bottom left: Sheppy the dog.

For a few years, I had a pet chicken. It had a crossed beak and seemed to stay away from the other chickens. I would pick it up and balance it on a stick which I held in front of me. It was very tame. I called it Henrietta until I determined it was a Henry!

Janet with her pet chicken Henry.

For several years, Dorothy and I enjoyed ice-skating on a small pond by the barn. We helped Daddy shovel off the snow and endured some very cold days. I remember going to Kokesh Hardware in Hopkins where we bought our first ice-skates. Later we went to a Skate Exchange in Minneapolis where we could trade the skates we had outgrown for bigger ones. Over the years, we spent many winter days skating on the pond or at school rinks. I loved to skate backwards! Once, when Dorothy and I were in our early teens, she took a hard fall on the ice, saw stars, and may have briefly lost consciousness. After that it seemed we lost interest in ice-skating and found other things to do.

As kids, Dorothy and I also went skiing down the hill on the south side of the house. It had just enough of a slope to get some speed before coming to a stop by the barn. I still have my old skis and it is comical to look at them. They are made of wood and a little more than five feet long with a leather strap where the boot slipped in. We also had a toboggan and sled to help us enjoy the cold Minnesota winters.

Janet's wooden skis used in early 1950s.

In the 1950s, I had my own flower garden on the south side of the house, near the entrance to the raspberry patch. It was on a spot where there had been a small chicken coop years before, so the soil was well fertilized. Daddy plowed it for me every spring, and I had rows of beautiful balsams, sylvias, zinnias, and gladioli. As a family, flowers were important to us, and Mother always had a row or two in her garden. Once my parents moved to another house, Mother had a round flower bed with the old green water pump displayed in the center. She tended it carefully, being sure the flowers had enough water throughout the summer. Daddy also took an interest in the flowers and helped with the watering.

In the 1950s, home permanents gained popularity. Getting a permanent in a hair salon was a luxury, so Mother became very proficient at giving home permanents to herself, Dorothy, and me. She bought the necessary rollers for winding the hair and the boxed permanent with end papers and two types of solutions. One solution was for the perm, and the other was the neutralizer. She gave us perms in the summer when she could keep the windows and doors open, as the smell permeated the house. She was always very careful not to get the solution on our skin. Once the perm was finished, she washed the rollers and stored them for future perms. Occasionally, she gave her sister-in-law Mabel a perm too. Mother kept up to date on the latest brand of perms. The perm Lilt was a favorite of hers for several years.

Dorothy and I both enjoyed keeping an account of our money. We had little notebooks in which we entered our allowance and the money we earned picking berries. We also kept track of our expenses: pencils, coloring books, and paper. Our parents encouraged us in this. They also started bank accounts for us, and we each had our own bank book.

We would save much of our berry picking money, and then go with Mother or Daddy to deposit it in the bank in Hopkins. The bank president, being of Czech heritage, knew nearly everyone in town and would greet us when we came in. Hopkins still had a large,

Janet's bank books.

friendly Czech population in the 1940s and 1950s, which owned many of the local businesses like the hardware store, dry cleaner, tailor, jeweler, and drugstore. My parents knew the owners of these stores and enjoyed a sense of camaraderie doing business with them as well as the assurance of getting an honest deal.

At some point, music became important to our family. Both Dorothy and I took piano lessons for several years. Initially, Daddy drove us to a teacher in Hopkins on Saturdays. When that got in the way of farm work, Mother found a teacher who would come to the house. He brought music books to sell so that we didn't have to find a place to buy them. I can still see him going through his briefcase searching for the appropriate books for us. Unfortunately, he never paid attention to our fingering, so to this day, I tend to get into trouble when I run out of fingers while playing!

In addition to the piano, Dorothy started to play the violin. Her first lesson was on May 12, 1951, when she was 13 years old. Mother's sister Sylvia played the violin with the St. Paul Chamber Orchestra, and I think this motivated Dorothy to start. She and I enjoyed playing piano-violin duets.

Summer meant berry picking. As long as I can remember, we always had patches of various sizes of both strawberries and raspberries. Strawberry season usually lasted through June, tapering off near the end of the month. At one time we also had a small patch of everbearing strawberries which bore in both the spring and fall, but mostly we grew strawberries that produced only in the spring. Raspberry season began in early July. Dorothy and Mother tied for being the fastest berry pickers in our family. I also picked but couldn't stand the mid-day sun as well as Dorothy. My face would get beet red, and I would feel a pounding in my head. Mother thought I got overheated when small and believed it happened one very hot day when we walked home from the sanatorium. After that day, I never tolerated the sun as well as before. So I helped crate berries or assisted Mother with meals. She and Daddy were always very protective of me and made sure I came in when it got hot to avoid the possibility of getting overheated again.

In the early 1950s, before we had a lot of our own raspberries, Dorothy went to pick raspberries for Mr. and Mrs. Neumeister who lived about a half mile away. She rode her bike down Baker Road to their house. During the peak of the season, Mother and I would also go help. The Neumeisters had a lot of raspberries and hired several berry pickers. Frank and Mary Neumeister were Czech, and both spoke the language fluently. Mary had a stocky build and curly red hair that framed her round, Czech face. I remember her speaking Czech a mile a minute and laughing with a Czech neighbor as they picked berries. Her cheeks were bright red and sweat poured down her face as she mopped it with a handkerchief. The Neumeisters were wonderful people and very good to Dorothy, appreciating her hard work. They treated her like the daughter they never had.

Our parents paid us well for picking berries. They appreciated our hard work and our ability to pick without squeezing and smashing the berries as was often the case with inexperienced pickers. We also knew which berries needed to be left to ripen more and which had insect bites or were soft and had to be thrown away.

Both Dorothy and I took driver's ed in school and had our first experience on the road. Daddy also took us out in our family car to get more experience before we took our driver's test. We practiced on rarely travelled roads and in vacant parking lots. Daddy always said that teaching us how to drive turned his hair grey! There was only one unfortunate incident during our training. Dorothy was driving home and made a right turn into our driveway which had two big cement posts, one on either side. She didn't quite turn the wheel far enough, and the left side of the car smashed into the cement post, taking out the headlight and part of the fender. Neither she nor Daddy, in the passenger seat, was injured. Dorothy of course felt terrible. Daddy was upset but didn't get angry. The car was drivable, so he took it to the dealer in Hopkins for repairs, and we all tried to forget what had happened. Dorothy went up to her room and painted her fingernails bright red to get her mind off the accident.

I vividly remember taking driver's ed. Even in a car with an automatic shift—not that common in the 1950s—I always had trouble parallel parking on level ground, let alone on a hill. As a result, I failed my first driver's test. On the second try, I passed with an 88 but still lost points on parking between cars. At that time, you could get your license at 15 and a half years old. I passed my test on August 24, 1956.

Dorothy and I got along very well, with few arguments, but when we did have disagreements, Mother found a way to solve them. For example, Dorothy and I had a shortage of wire hangers for our clothes, and we used to fight over unclaimed hangers. So Mother divided all the hangers in half, and Dorothy tied a green string on hers, and I tied a red string on mine. A similar problem happened with pillowcases that got mixed up in the laundry. Dorothy sewed a green thread on hers, and I sewed a red thread on mine. Problem solved!

14. DOROTHY AND JANET: SCHOOL DAYS

Our school year always started the day after Labor Day. For many, Labor Day was the last day of vacation, but for our family, it was the last free day to get chores done. Dorothy and I often had a new dress to wear on the first day of school. Our dresses usually needed to be shortened and on Labor Day, we would finish hemming them. We each had our own room, which we cleaned the day before going back to school. Finally, we assembled our school supplies: pencils, paper, notebooks, eraser, ruler, and binders. We always joked that it truly was a day of labor!

We went to Eden Prairie Consolidated School for all 12 grades. The large, reddish-brown, brick building sat on a hill and as the student population grew, a wing for grades 8 through 12 was added in the 1950s. The school offered a half-day kindergarten, but students had to be picked up at noon or brought at noon for the afternoon class. Neither Dorothy nor I could attend kindergarten because a trip in the middle of the day would have been too much of an interruption of Daddy's farm work.

The school had four buses, each with its own route. They lined up outside the school at the end of the day, and we would hurry to get on and get a seat by the window. We had a 15- to 20-minute ride in the morning, getting on the bus at 8:10 a.m., and a 35- to 45-minute ride in the afternoon getting home at 4:30 p.m. We could see the bus through the trees on what is now 62nd Street when it came in

Eden Prairie Consolidated School which Dorothy and Janet attended for grades 1 through 12.

the morning. It had to stop at the corner before turning right and heading toward our stop. We got on the bus at the end of our driveway which meant we had about three minutes to get to the stop once we saw the bus through the trees. The bus kept to its schedule, and I remember running to get the bus if we were a bit late in the morning. Sometimes, the bus driver pretended he didn't see us running, and he would go right on by. He stopped and waited for us, greeting us with a good laugh. We waited for the bus by the stone pillars at the end of our driveway, using them to protect us from the wind or the sun on hot days. When it was raining or especially cold, Daddy took us down in the car and waited with us at the end of the driveway until the bus came. I never minded the bus ride and enjoyed sitting and talking with friends or just looking out the window. On occasion, when the kids got too noisy or rowdy, the bus driver would stop and tell us to "settle down." We had no identifying badges to keep track of who was getting on and off the bus as kids do today.

Road Dorothy and Janet walked down to catch school bus.

The bus always stopped before railroad crossings, and one of the boys would get out, look both ways, and flag the bus across the tracks. The same student usually did this, but if he were absent, any boy could volunteer. This was in the days before railroad crossing barriers and was an extra precaution to avoid the bus from being hit by a train. There were about four of these crossings on our bus route.

On the ride home, our bus turned a corner at Chanhassen, which at the time was just a small community of about 200 people. We never would have guessed that Chanhassen would gain such fame in the 1980s as the home of Prince and his 65,000-square-foot complex, Paisley Park. Thousands of Prince's fans tour this site annually to see his studio, concert hall, exhibits, and personal archives. Earlier, in 1968, Chanhassen's Dinner Theatre opened and gained fame with its concert series, Broadway shows, and excellent dining.

After the turn at Chanhassen, the bus continued its route on rural roads, stopping at students' driveways. There was no common stopping point like today. The bus driver always put out the stop sign on the left side of the bus, first checking to make sure no cars were zipping by, because students often had to cross the road in front of the bus.

Mother made our school lunches, although we could buy a hot meal in school for $0.20. Occasionally, we bought the school lunch if we liked what was on the published menu, but there were no choices. Mother made us a variety of sandwiches with ham or jelly; she would also fry hamburgers or cook hotdogs. She always added an orange or apple, carrots or celery sticks and, in the fall, small yellow tomatoes, a favorite of mine. For dessert, she put in cookies or cake and if she didn't have these, she would stir up frosting with powdered sugar and milk and spread it between two graham crackers. We had metal lunch buckets with a thermos of water or juice. I always enjoyed these lunches, even though they were cold.

At school, we ate on the bleachers overlooking the gym floor. Those who managed to get in the lunch room first sat at a few tables above the bleachers. One of the tables was always reserved for the teachers and superintendent, who ate at the same time as the students and kept a watchful eye on us.

Several steps led to the front entrance of the school where the buses stopped. A short hall with administrative offices was right inside the entrance. It also had a place where we could buy school supplies like pencils, paper, and erasers. This short hall led to a long hallway extending to the right and left horizontally. The building had two restrooms, one for girls on the left at the end of the hall with 10 stalls and 6 sinks, and one for the boys at the other end of the hall.

Classrooms lined the hallway on both sides with the lower grades to the left and the upper grades to the right. Each classroom had a cloakroom in the back for our coats and boots. There were five rows of about eight desks. Each row of desks was permanently attached to the floor. The desks had a writing surface that could be raised with a place underneath to keep our notebooks, pencils, loose papers, worksheets, and other supplies. Sometimes, this could get quite messy, and we would have a designated time to clean our desks. We had assigned seats. Occasionally, a change would be made in the seating chart if a student had trouble seeing the blackboard, or if there were behavioral problems.

Radiators lined the classroom wall which kept the room warm but had an annoying clanging sound from time to time. I remember one time a student took one of the few chairs from the front of the room to sit next to the radiator. Trying to get warm, he tipped the chair back and it slipped. He fell, hitting his head on the radiator, and blood spewed everywhere. Fortunately, he was not seriously hurt.

The occasional discipline problem meant either a trip to the principal's office or a more immediate solution by an individual teacher. Teachers would tape a student's mouth shut or escort the student to the bathroom to physically wash out the student's mouth with soap for using foul language. I never witnessed this as it was usually a boy taken to the boys' bathroom. One teacher both Dorothy

180 | *Life on a Czech Farm in Minnesota*

and I had in eighth grade had few discipline problems in her class because she met them with immediate action. She would stomp down the row to the misbehaving student, grab him—always a boy—by the hair and shake his head, then slap him on one cheek, then the other, talking the whole time. She shook him by the hair again, stormed back up to the front of the room, and continued the lesson. Whew…no one wanted to be on the receiving end of that.

We received report cards every six weeks which had to be taken home, signed by a parent, and returned to school. The cards came in a four-by-six inch, tan envelope and listed the subjects taken and the grades for a six-week period. At the end of the school year, our teacher gave us our report card to keep. I have saved all of mine!

Janet's report cards for grades 3 and 9, and a perfect attendance certificate for 1951-1952.

Our class took several field trips each year, which I thoroughly enjoyed because our family rarely went places that were not connected to the farm. I remember visiting a candy factory and being fascinated while watching women put the curl on top of chocolates manually with a flick of their finger. We also visited the *Minneapolis Tribune*, the Franklin Creamery, and an artificial limb factory. At the end of the year, the classes went on a picnic. A favorite place was Minnehaha Falls. As kids, we scrambled over the hills and rocks like mountain goats and had squirt gun fights until we were drenched.

The fear of polio spread in the 1940s to the mid-1950s. Though school was never cancelled, we all recognized the need to take sanitary measures seriously. One student in my high school class contracted polio. I remember him as a chunky, happy kid who suddenly disappeared from school. Almost a year later, he returned, very thin and with a scar on his throat. He had a very deep, hard to understand voice as a result of his treatment for polio. The fear of contracting polio continued until the Salk vaccine became available in the mid-1950s.[39]

Our years at Eden Prairie were full of mostly good memories, but one wound I'll never forget was not being chosen for Girls' State. Schools statewide chose one junior girl to attend a weeklong educational program where they held a mock government to teach how government works. Dorothy had gone to Girls' State as a junior and had a wonderful experience. We didn't have many outside experiences, so this was very special. Two boys and I were the class leaders when it came to politics and current events. In study hall, the three of us would have contests naming countries and capitals. One of these students and I even won a prize in a current events contest. So I thought, given my interest in current events, surely I would be chosen for Girls' State. But it did not happen. Instead, another girl was selected, and I was the alternate. I was crushed and terribly disappointed.

Major events in the school year included a carnival in the fall. One of the big attractions was the dunking board. Teachers often volunteered to lie on the board attached to a device that when hit by a ball thrower, tipped the board and dunked the teacher in a tank of water. The carnival had the usual chance games for prizes of stuffed animals and glitzy items. I remember Senator Hubert Humphrey attended once, and his presence drew a large crowd as he walked through, smiling and shaking hands.

Homecoming also attracted a large crowd. There was a basketball game, the coronation of King and Queen, and sometimes a talent show, followed by a dance with a live band. I have fond memories of a bunch of us in junior high doing the schottische (which took four dancers) and the polka as we careened around the floor among the more serious dancers. Dorothy and I performed in several talent shows. When I was seven or eight, I did a tap dance at a talent show, and the MC Sev Widman asked if he could do it with me. That startled me, but somehow I managed to get through it.

Once at a baton-twirling program, I had the honor of twirling a lighted baton. I was a bit nervous when all the lights went out, and

Janet tap dancing with MC Sev Widman at a school talent show.

I was alone on the stage, but it was one of the highlights of my school days. When I was a senior, I auditioned and got the role as Mistress of Ceremonies, which I surprisingly enjoyed once my nerves settled down.

At another talent show, Dorothy and I played a piano-violin duet, and we played the piano for other school events, like graduation. This was an experience I enjoyed for several years. I was also the accompanist for our high school choir and still remember the fear I had of making a mistake as I played the introduction. I would rather have just sung in the choir!

Juniors and seniors put on a class play every year, and Dorothy and I both participated in these. As a junior, I played Eloise

Dorothy playing violin in a piano-violin duet with Janet at the Homecoming talent show, 1954.

Hotchkiss—a fairly minor role—in *A Date with Judy*. As a senior, I had a more substantial role as Beth in *Little Women*.

Dorothy and I also worked on the school newspaper, *The Eden Prairie Buzzer*. We were on the staff for several years and as seniors were co-editors in our respective years. I remember going to local businesses to ask them to place an ad in the paper to support its cost. Most businesses gladly contributed.

The main sport in school was basketball. Daddy took us to watch weekend games and picked us up after. Sometimes, a parent of one of our friends would give us a ride instead. The games with neighboring schools Chaska, Shakopee, Waconia, Prior Lake, Orono, Watertown, and Burnsville were exciting. We always cheered for Harold Duda, one of my classmates who played on the team. Students paid $0.25 and adults $0.75 for admission.

Once our friends could drive, we went to shows and roller-skating. Dorothy's best friend, Karen Sorenson, lived just a couple of miles away. They often went places together and on occasion, Karen and her sister Rachel—a year younger than me—helped us pick berries.

My best friend, Karen Brown, often picked me up to go to a movie or roller-skating. Karen drove a Ford that got frequent vapor locks, leaving us stranded until the car started again. My friends included Bobby Kopesky and George Holasek. Bobby and I had frequent political debates. We both loved history and would talk at length about historical figures. Eventually, he went to Hamline University and taught history in Jefferson County, Colorado. When I worked in Estes Park the summer of 1961, I visited him in Denver.

Our school days ended in the 1950s. Dorothy graduated on June 3, 1955 with 13 in her class, and I graduated in 1958 with a class of 26. Overall, we enjoyed our school years and both of us felt prepared for the future. We had worked hard and both of us graduated as valedictorians of our class. Throughout our school days, Mother and Daddy encouraged us to get good grades and were proud of our achievements. Giving our valedictorian speeches was a bittersweet moment for both Dorothy and me as we reflected on our experiences of the last 12 years.

Janet (third from the left) and her Eden Prairie high-school graduation class, 1958.

15. THE SWITCH TO CHICKENS AND BERRIES

In the early 1950s, Mother and Daddy contemplated the switch from cows to chickens due to the well problem and expensive equipment changes affecting milk production. They also planned to increase the size of the strawberry and raspberry patches, figuring that the income from egg production and berries would be sufficient for living expenses. This was not an easy decision because it meant more work year round for both of them. They had to build a brooder house for baby chicks and renovate the cow barn for the chickens to live in once they became laying hens. The transition began in 1953 and from 1954 through 1960, they depended on these new sources of income (see chart of income and expenses on page 204).

In 1953, they started the transition by building a brooder house, a building in which to raise the baby chicks. The materials for it cost $325 and the 200 baby chicks cost $136. Mother and Daddy fenced in the grassy area around the brooder house so the chickens had free range once they were old enough to go outside.

In May 1954, my parents sold the cows and began converting the basement of the barn into a chicken coop where laying hens would be kept. They remodeled the barn by themselves, a physically difficult job without the power tools available today. I can still picture Mother, red-faced, laboring over sawing a two-by-four with a hand saw. They took out the cow stanchions and redid the floor.

They filled the gutters, which had been behind the cows, with cement. They covered the floor with straw and built rows of nests and a huge roost where the chickens went at night.

On September 2, 1954, the fiberglass insulation arrived. This had to be installed throughout the basement of the barn to keep it warm enough for the chickens in the winter. Fortuitously, David Pinks, a former hired hand, had stopped in for one of his occasional visits and volunteered to help with its installation. My folks greatly appreciated his help over several days. It took a tremendous amount of work with a material cost of $534.43. In addition, my parents spent $245 on an electric fan to provide air circulation for the laying hens, and $135 on a corn sheller to replace the hand crank one they had been using. This was one of Mother's top priorities in the conversion! They spent $263.70 on chicken equipment and $313.75 to purchase 500 baby chicks. In 1954, they saw their first significant income from eggs: $1,343.53.

Mother had the responsibility of tending the 500 chicks which my parents bought in the spring. The brooder house was within 200 feet of our house, making it convenient for her to check on the chicks frequently. My parents went to New Prague to buy the chicks and brought them home in huge cardboard boxes. I remember helping take them out of the boxes, each one just a handful of yellow fluff, making cheeping sounds. They required constant attention, from keeping the feeding troughs and drinking jars filled, to watching for illness in the flock. The drinking devices were large glass jars tipped upside down into saucer-like holders, allowing a steady stream of water. I often went with Mother when she checked on the feed and water and marveled at how she tipped the heavy water jars upside down to flow into the saucers. For the first several weeks, the brooder house had heat lamps to keep the chicks warm until they grew feathers.

Mother always had to be alert to problems, one being the appearance of blood on the tail of a growing chicken. Chickens will target another chicken and harass it by pecking at it and drawing blood. Blood attracts other chickens, and they would mercilessly chase and peck the chicken to death if Mother didn't catch it in time. To alleviate this problem, she used a special red ointment which had a nasty taste and was made especially for this purpose. She would catch 10 to 15 chickens that did not have blood on their tails and wipe the red ointment on them. The chickens would go after these marked ones thinking it was blood, but after getting a taste of the bitter ointment, they stopped the pecking. In appearance, they could not tell the difference between blood and the ointment.

In the evenings, Mother made sure to shut the small doors that allowed the chickens to go outside into the fenced-in area during the day. There was always the danger that a fox or other animal could jump the fence and get at the chickens in the brooder house. During Mother's last check on the chickens, she made sure they had settled down for the night. On occasion, they seemed restless due to a barking dog or thunderstorm. Chickens are intelligent and can sense danger. Mother could calm them down by quietly talking to them.

At the end of August, the chickens had to be transferred from the brooder house to the basement of the barn. My parents spent several days preparing the barn for this. Nests had to be cleaned and filled with fresh straw or hay to protect the eggs, the floor needed to be covered with fresh straw, and repairs made to the roost. Feeding troughs and watering jars also had to be cleaned and filled.

The barn was divided into several sections. One part held the laying hens from the previous year while two other sections held young chickens brought from the brooder house. When all was ready, Mother and Daddy hand-carried 500, close-to-laying hens to the basement. This transfer took at least two days. It meant carrying chickens, two at a time, from the brooder house to the barn, down 14 cement steps, gently putting the chickens down, climbing back up the 14 steps, and returning to the brooder house for two more chickens. That amounted to over 100 trips a day! They had to watch closely to make sure the chickens settled down in their new home. After two years, the production of a laying hen would begin to wane, and she would be sold to Johnson's Produce Market to be turned into good soup meat.

In the spring, the cycle started over with preparations for the baby chickens. Mother cleaned the brooder house if it had not been done in the fall. She brought in fresh straw for the floor and filled the feeding troughs and watering jars. About mid-April, my parents would go to New Prague and purchase 500 new chicks. Once again, Mother kept a close watch on them to make sure they started eating and drinking.

Holasek farm with chickens, corn crib, and granary (left), silo next to barn (right), 1956.

It took considerable time to gather hundreds of eggs each day and prepare them to be sold commercially. Like berry picking, this engaged the whole family. While strict licensing was not required as today, tax returns for 1957 show the beginning of a $5 charge for an egg license. Care had to be taken to ensure that the eggs were handled safely. My parents purchased special wire baskets to use in gathering eggs from the nests. These baskets permitted air flow to cool the eggs. Once filled, they were carried to the basement in the house where it was cool.

We all spent many hours, usually in the evening, preparing the eggs for market. First, the eggs had to be cleaned by removing any dirt with a special handheld sandpaper cleaner, much like those used to sand wood. Water could not be used, as it would take the protective coating off the egg. The eggs had to be candled, which

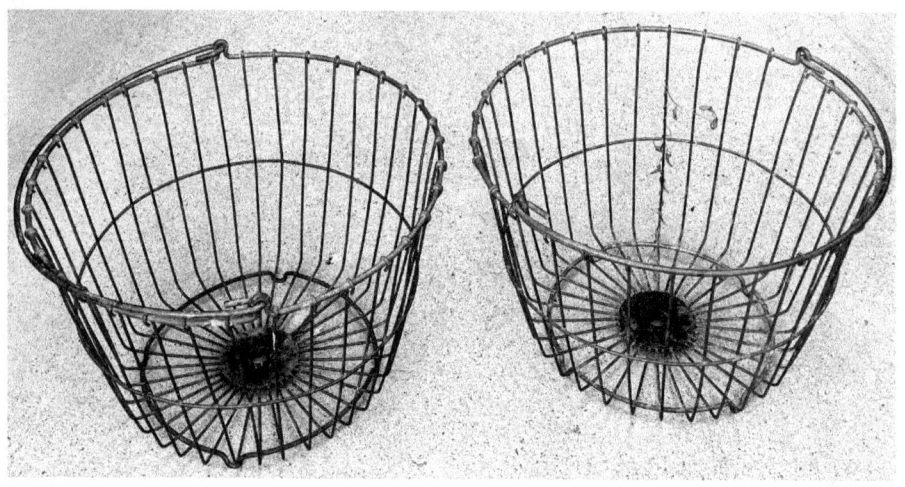

Wire baskets used to gather eggs.

Mother and Daddy did. The candling device allowed them to hold each egg in front of a light to detect any blood spots or unusual yolk or white formations. They placed the rejects in separate cartons, and Mother used them for baking and our breakfasts. Of course, eggs that looked particularly bad were thrown out. But, for years, the only eggs we ate were the rejects. A tiny speck of blood made no difference in the egg's taste and was a natural occurrence in the egg's formation, but such eggs could not go into the public market. After eating fresh eggs from home, it took me many years before I could eat eggs in a restaurant. They just didn't taste the same.

In the first two years, 1953 and 1954, my parents sold the eggs to grocery stores in Glen Lake and Hopkins, like Kraemers, Country Club, and Hovanders. They also sold to friends and relatives who came to the house. Mother's sister Gloria and her family came every week. But as egg production increased, Daddy thought a better price could be obtained by going door to door to get scheduled customers. He decided they would look for customers in upscale neighborhoods where families welcomed the opportunity to get fresh farm eggs. Unfortunately, that job fell to Mother who had to go door to door, first to get customers, and then to deliver the eggs. Daddy drove and sat in the car. Their first day of "peddling" eggs, as Mother put it, was December 8, 1954. Mother remembered it as the worst time of her life, especially on cold winter days. Women would come to the door, and she would look into their nice warm houses while the wind and snow blew on her. She had to take her mittens off to make change and write orders for the next week in her notebook. Fingers numbed from the cold, she would drop coins and barely be able to write. She felt like a beggar going door to door and often thought that the women bought eggs because they felt sorry for her standing out in the cold. It was embarrassing and humiliating.

I am not sure how long they continued what they called the egg route but fortunately, sometime during the next year 1955, they learned that Red Owl grocery would buy their eggs if put in Red Owl cartons. It was a godsend for Mother who no longer had to peddle eggs. Red Owl provided a machine to make the cartons. Daddy fastened the machine to a table in the basement, and I made most of the cartons. Sitting on a chair, I simply put the flattened carton on the machine, matched notches, pulled down a handle, and the carton was formed. I weighed the cleaned and candled eggs, making sure they met the required 2 to 2 ¼ ounces for large eggs, and put them in the cartons of a dozen each. I placed the filled cartons into the large Red Owl cases, each holding 24 dozen. The case had a divider in

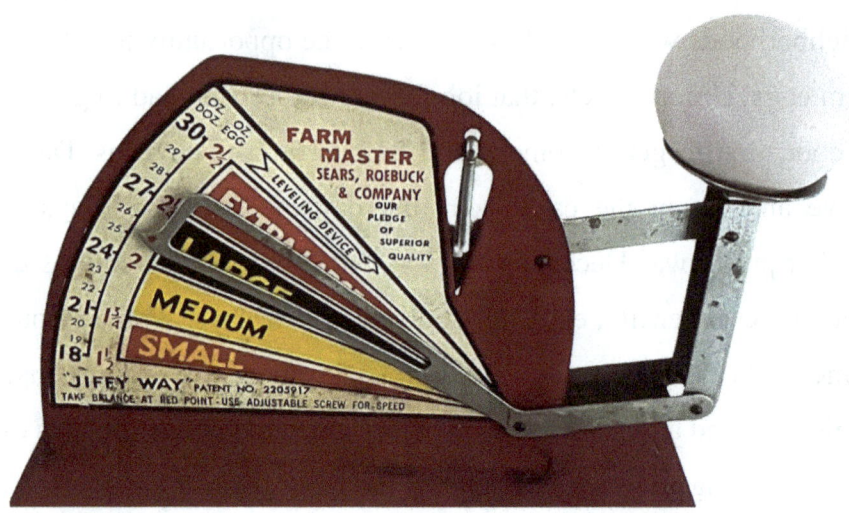

Egg scale used by Holasek family, 1950s.

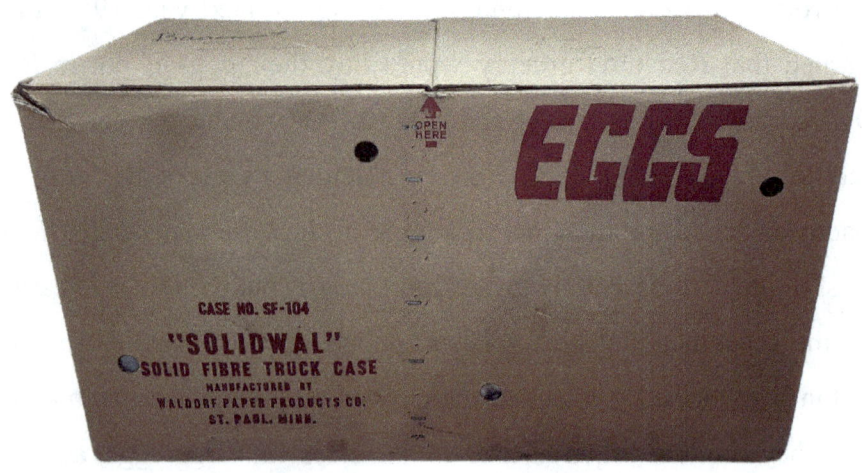

Red Owl egg case holding 24 dozen eggs.

the middle so that each side held 12 dozen. I still have two of these cases, which I have used for moving and as storage boxes!

After graduating from high school in 1958, I worked as a secretary for two years at Honeywell Ordnance Division in Hopkins to earn money for college. In the evenings, I helped prepare eggs for market by cleaning them and making cartons. Dorothy went to business college after graduating from high school in 1955, but when she came home on weekends, she helped us. Once a week, Daddy loaded the cases into the car, and Mother and I delivered the eggs to Red Owl. I drove and pulled up to the loading dock at the back of the store. Mother went to get a clerk who unloaded the cases, giving us a slip for payment. This was my small contribution for living at home and not paying rent while working and saving money for college.

Back in 1953, my parents had planted large patches of raspberries and strawberries to bring in additional income. They always had some berries for our own use to freeze for the coming winter, and, to sell at roadside stands at the peak of the season. Daddy had connections with fruit and vegetable stands on Highway 7, often with Czech owners who knew the high quality of our berries. When planting, my parents estimated how large a patch our family would be able to handle, except at the peak of the season when we would get neighbors and relatives to help pick berries. Dorothy, Mother, and Daddy were the champion berry pickers. I did well as long as the weather wasn't too hot. In 1954, income from berries brought in $858.92. The following year, it reached over $2,000.

Using 1956 as a typical year (based on my diary for 1956),

Raspberry patch on Holasek farm, 1956.

View of raspberry patch on Holasek farm, 1973.

strawberry season began mid-June. The patch was not adjacent to the house, but in the back woods where the cows had pastured. Early in the morning, Daddy drove us there in the truck. It was less than a 5-minute ride but a 15-minute walk from the house. The strawberry leaves still had dew drops. We had no hired help, so just the four of us had to cover the whole patch. The strawberries grew in rows, and each row was about two to three feet wide with hay between the rows. Picking was best done either from a bent-over position, until the back gave out, or from a kneeling position with one person on each side of the row. We crawled along the hay between the rows, on our knees, getting wet, looking for ripe berries among the dew-drenched leaves. Each berry had to be checked to see if it was ripe enough and, if so, you snapped the stem to separate the berry from the plant. Some berries had soft spots or bug bites and had to be left or thrown out. Our long sleeves, which protected us from mosquitoes, got soaked as deer flies and mosquitoes hovered around us, making picking miserable. We each had a wooden carrier with six quart boxes which we pushed or placed between the rows as we picked. When filled, we took the carrier to the truck parked nearby and used for crating. We took out the full quarts of berries and put empty boxes in their place and returned to the patch. Often, Daddy would be there to help, as he was in charge of crating the berries.

Mosquitoes made us miserable. They flew into our eyes, ears, and around our head. Daddy made a smudge to see if the smoke would keep them away, and it helped a bit. To try to keep them away, we sewed mosquito netting around the rim of our straw hats. Once, I held my hat over the smoke from the smudge to get extra protection, hoping the smell of smoke would keep the mosquitoes away, but suddenly, the net burst into flames and was gone in an instant. Fortunately, I wasn't wearing it at the time!

We took occasional breaks mid-morning and mid-afternoon. I always had a Baby Ruth candy bar for a mid-morning snack, which I later blamed for the cavity I got in my front tooth! Daddy would get day-old pastries at the grocery store until, one day, I found a huge dead bug embedded in my pastry. We found other snacks after that!

On June 17, 1956, we picked the first strawberries, filling half a crate (12 quart boxes). On June 20, we picked 2 crates. On June 22, production increased to 8 crates plus 12 quarts. Strawberries increased in the following days, June 24, 25, and 26. It rained on June 26, but we picked between showers. We picked every day through July 2, except on June 30. Despite occasional showers, we picked on July 4 and 5. The constant rain made the mosquitoes worse, and nothing kept them away. Gradually, the berries tapered off, and July 6 was close to our last day.

Every day, Daddy took the full crates to the Excelsior Fruit Growers Association, where he had taken berries back in the 1930s! But as a harbinger of things to come, the Association dissolved in 1969, as fruit production had declined in the area due to farmers selling land to the increasing demands of creeping urbanization. The Association closed at 5:00 p.m., so Daddy had to leave by around 4:15–4:30 p.m. Sometimes, I went with him and, in early July, while in Excelsior, he purchased a load of raspberry crates to prepare for their production. All raspberry and strawberry crates and boxes were wooden. During this brief period between the end of strawberry picking and the beginning of raspberry picking, my parents cleaned the chicken coops, shelled corn, hoed in the garden, while doing the daily work of feeding and tending the now 1,000 chickens and, in the evening, preparing the eggs for sale. It was a very busy time!

The raspberry crop in 1956 began in early July. The first picking of raspberries was July 8, and the last picking of strawberries was on July 9. The raspberry patch was adjacent to the house so we could go in quickly for a snack or drink of water. Another advantage was that raspberries were much easier to pick. The raspberry bushes were planted in rows of about 40 bushes. As they often grew to five to five-and-a-half feet, we stood while picking, and the carriers had legs making it easy to put the berries in the boxes. Raspberries were put in pint boxes, not quarts like strawberries. Each raspberry carrier held six boxes. As with strawberries, there was one person on each side of the row, or a person would pick one side, and then the other. We avoided walking around the bush because going between bushes could break the branches. When our carrier was full, we took it to the truck, parked under a tree close to the patch. We either took out the full boxes and replaced them with empties, or Daddy would help us with it when there.

Raspberry production lasted about a month. We picked every day through August 7, except for July 21 and 30. If it rained, we sat it out. We went back out when it stopped even though the berries would be wet and our clothes would get soaked from the dripping bushes. Unlike strawberries that are on a stem, raspberries are pulled off a hull. One had to be careful not to hold too many in the hand so they wouldn't get squashed. Also, some that were not well formed crumbled and needed to be dropped on the ground. Mosquitoes still bothered us in the early morning, but since we stood while picking, it was more tolerable. At the peak of production in 1956, July 18 and 19, we had neighbors and relatives helping us. We could not go to the Raspberry Parade on July 29 because we had our own raspberry festival picking berries! Gradually, raspberry production declined and, as of August 7, we picked every other day until August 14 which was our last day.

As with the strawberries, Daddy took the raspberries to the Excelsior Fruit Growers Association. However, we never finished picking by the time he had to leave before the Association closed, so he arranged to sell raspberries to fruit stands along Highway 7. He took berries to the stands of Mr. Hanus and Mr. Kvetensky, and other stands known as Brom's and High View. Our berries always had a good reputation for not being crumbly or squeezed, so he had no trouble finding a market for them. This meant that we would continue picking well into the evening, which made for very long days.

At the peak of the season, we picked from dawn until dusk. On one particularly busy day, Dorothy ran out of the raspberry patch screaming hysterically. It was late, about 7:00 p.m. She was tired from picking all day, and when she reached up for some berries, she almost grabbed a snake coiled around the wooden raspberry stake. Daddy immediately went out to the patch where she had been and returned to say she didn't have to worry about it anymore. From that moment on, she had a strong aversion to snakes, and no one could blame her.

Richard, c. 1960 (left), receipt from Excelsior Fruit Growers Association for 25.5 crates of raspberries, 1956 (right).

In the fall, the berry canes had to be covered to prevent them from freezing. Mother bent down the raspberry canes while Daddy plowed dirt over them, just as they had done in the 1920s. They covered the strawberries with hay hauled from the haystack. Sometimes, this was done as late as mid-November.

The berries could now be left until the spring when they needed to be uncovered. Hay or straw was removed from the strawberries and placed between the rows, making picking easier. Uncovering the raspberries involved more work. Dirt was removed from the bent-over canes, and Mother, carrying a ball of twine, tied the new canes of each bush in three places. For the next three months, Daddy would plow between the rows and hoe around each bush to keep the soil loose and weed free. It was a matter of pride to keep berries and garden areas clean or free from weeds.

Strawberry carrier repurposed for Janet's grandchildren's art supplies.

Raspberry carrier repurposed for plants.

The years of raising chickens for egg production along with the strawberries and raspberries were probably the busiest years for my parents. In the summer, the garden crops also needed tending and had to be preserved for the winter. Corn needed to be shelled for the chickens along with mixing their feed, plus the daily work of preparing the eggs for market.

A look at the income and expenses in the 1950s, taken from income tax reports, is helpful for learning how much was made from egg and berry production. Raising chickens was expensive, and expenses often equaled half (or more than half) of what was earned from the sale of eggs. There was no way to reduce the expenses. As it was, my parents did all the work themselves, from renovating the barn to preparing eggs for market. Necessary and unavoidable expenses were limited to the purchase of baby chicks, feed, and equipment. Also, the price of a dozen eggs was unpredictable, fluctuating greatly and ranging from $0.57 in 1955 to $0.37 in 1959.

Berry income, on the other hand, had few expenses, as it mainly required labor of the family. The only unavoidable expenses were the boxes and crates and, during the peak of the season, extra pickers. Plants for new patches of strawberries and raspberries came from the existing plants and involved no extra cost.

Another source of income in the 1950s was alfalfa. Since Mother and Daddy no longer needed this hay as food for the cows, they sold it, seeing their income from hay rise from $80 in 1954 to $549.23 in 1962.

YEARLY INCOME & CHICKEN EXPENSES (1953-1971)

Year	Income Chickens/ Eggs	Expenses Chickens	Income Berries	Income Hay/Oats/ Corn
1953	$326.37	$639.38	None	None
1954	$1,343.53	$1,491.88	$858.92	$80.00
1955	$4,146.45	$1,893.87	$2,130.04	$70.00
1956	$4,584.89	$2,654.95	$1,215.07	$431.68
1957	$6,423.10	$3,230.51	$1,242.60	$346.70
1958	$3,892.58	$2,152.94	$2,245.00	$403.50
1959	$3,715.53	$2,485.66	$2,375.64	$267.00
1960	$3,767.10	$1,425.55	$2,447.00	$393.45
1961	$864.33	$333.52	$2,676.75	$451.90
1962	None	None	$2,764.00	$549.23
1963	None	None	$1,815.00	$230.00
1964	None	None	$2,195.00	None
1965	None	None	$1,673.00	None
1966	None	None	$1,810.00	None
1967	None	None	$985.31	None
1968	None	None	$1,108.45	None
1969	None	None	$1,600.00	None
1970	None	None	$1,461.00	None
1971	None	None	$1,638.00	None

My parents continued marketing eggs and berries throughout the 1950s, managing to make a reasonably good income until 1960 when they stopped raising chickens and bought no baby chicks that year. In the final two years, 1958 and 1959, chicken expenses were more than half the income from eggs, contributing to their decision to phase out egg production.

A bigger change was coming, however. Eden Prairie was no longer simply an agricultural community. Businesses, recreational establishments, and housing developments had started to encroach on farmland. In 1960, the state bought 26 acres of my parents' farmland which included the land of the major strawberry patch, for the proposed Interstate 494 highway. Over the next several years, the entire family farm was sold in piecemeal fashion, with the last piece being sold in 1989.

In 1960, I left home for college at Hamline University. Dorothy had started there in 1957. Also, in the fall of 1960, Mother —always eager to try something different—began to work as a clerk in Donaldson's Department store in Minneapolis. She worked only part time but wanted to get enough hours to qualify for Social Security. She loved to ride the bus to and from Minneapolis, and Daddy would take her and pick her up at the sanatorium. She enjoyed greeting and helping customers and, given her quick mind, it didn't take her long to learn how to make change and run the cash register.

Despite these changes, my parents continued to grow and market raspberries. The table on page 204 shows income from berries as late as 1971. They even started a new patch next to the house they moved to in 1967. The original farmhouse was at 6233 Baker Road and the new house was just down the road at 6375 Baker Road. Daddy had seen a pink house in Hopkins that he liked and decided on pink for the new house; Mother had no objection and was pleased with the color. Retirement years were ahead of them, but that still included working on the land where they loved growing berries, vegetables, and flowers.

16. FAMILY AND FRIENDS

Farm work and household chores occupied most of our time on the farm with outings to the grocery store, meat locker, hardware store, and other stores for basic necessities. Our entertainment came from listening to radio programs or watching television in the evenings, mainly in the winter. Most of our parents' family lived within a 20-minute drive, so they frequently came to visit us, or we went to visit them. That was the extent of our socializing.

Daddy's sisters stopped in occasionally. Mabel was known as Auntie Mickey by her nieces and as Babe by adults. She visited with her husband George Reuter and their son Dennis who entertained us playing his accordion—to his parents' delight. They often came for Daddy's birthday on March 1. Their younger son Roger was developmentally disabled and passed away in 1963.

Mabel took great pride in her blonde hair—always well coiffed—and the double strand pearl necklace that she wore every day. I remember evening visits to Aunt Mickey's in Hopkins, a short 20-minute drive which went by the Poor Farm supported by Hennepin County. The Poor Farm provided a place for those who depended on public support, often the elderly and people with disabilities. Men could be seen walking around the grounds, smoking or sitting and visiting with each other.

George and Mabel (Holasek) Reuter's wedding photo; standing left to right: Gladys Reuter (George's sister), Daniel Pry (best man), Hazel Holasek (Mabel's sister, maid of honor), July 28, 1934.

Dennis Reuter, 1958.

Holasek family's kerosene lamp converted to electric lamp.

Gravy boat (top), sugar and creamer used by Mabel (Holasek) Reuter.

Sometimes, the trip involved stopping for gas. An attendant would come up to the driver's window. Daddy would address him as "Yowser" which apparently was derived from "Yes sir." He would tell the attendant if he wanted the tank filled up or the oil checked. "Yowser" proceeded to wash the windows while the tank filled up. Daddy paid him in cash and never had to get out of the car. This service and personal exchange was common for the time but has been lost today as we fuel our own cars, wash our own windshields, and rarely talk to anyone.

Uncle George had a stroke in 1976 and went into a nursing home as a result. He passed away July 2, 1984. Dennis never married and died much too young in 1987 at the age of 47. Mabel had a couple of Certificates of Deposit worth several thousand dollars and asked Mother who she should put as beneficiaries, since both her sons were gone. Knowing Mabel's affection for her nieces, Mother suggested leaving them to Dorothy and me, which she did.

Mabel, now alone, often visited my parents and helped them pick berries. One fairly warm day in November 1987 when Mabel was visiting, she went to get our mail, a short 200-yard walk from the house. On the way back, she may have tripped and fell face down, but it appeared she actually had a sudden heart attack and was probably gone before she hit the ground. She was 81 years old.

Mabel and Daddy's older sister Hazel worked for a beauty shop in Hopkins. Before Mabel married George Reuter, she and Hazel lived together in an apartment in Hopkins. In the late 1920s, their parents John and Mary Holasek bought a bungalow-style house

John and Mary Holasek's house on 210 9th Avenue North in Hopkins.

at 210 9th Avenue North in Hopkins. Hazel and Mabel moved into it with them. As noted earlier, John and Mary had moved to Hopkins when their son Lilliard married Aimee in December 1928, leaving the farm to the newlyweds.

Hazel had a sharp tongue and didn't hesitate to berate others for no reason. Back in the 1920s, Mother remembers being on the receiving end of a tongue lashing. But Hazel's dad had overheard the tirade and let Hazel know that he never wanted to hear her say another unkind word to Evelyn. Mother said it made a difference in the way Hazel treated her. John, a kind and generous man, admired Evelyn and told her one time that no other woman came close to doing the work, both inside and outside the house, that she did.

Aunt Hazel was a fantastic cook, and I can still remember the wonderful aroma of her chicken soup. She had moved her work as a beautician to the basement of the house, and the smell of perms often wafted upstairs. Sometimes, Dorothy and I stayed overnight at her house. By that time, both her parents had died—John in 1936 and Mary in 1946. I was only six years old when Grandma Holasek died and have only a vague recollection of her.

In 1945, to everyone's surprise, Hazel at 48 years old married John "Jack" White, a kind, personable, jack-of-all-trades man who worked in the post office. Somehow, he put up with Hazel's unpredictable temperament and drove her wherever she wanted to go. Hazel loved to play Bingo, and Jack would drive her to games then return home and pick her up when she was finished.

They often came to visit us and would sit in the dining room, talking with us while we finished supper. Jack had several beehives in the woods. I remember going with him to check the hives and having my first taste of delicious cone honey. Mother recalls that Hazel once asked her which daughter she favored most. Mother was stunned by the question. How could a mother favor one child over the other? She reasoned that Hazel would never understand, having no children of her own.

On one occasion, probably in 1950, Daddy and Hazel got into an ugly argument. It had something to do with whether Dorothy and I would come and stay overnight at Hazel and Jack's and ended with Daddy saying that no one would tell him how to run his life! Hazel stormed out, Jack followed behind meekly, and they drove off. I don't know if Daddy and Hazel ever mended their relationship by the time Hazel died on February 5, 1974. Jack remarried the

John and Hazel (Holasek) White's wedding photo with Richard Holasek (left) and Mabel (Holasek) Reuter (right), November 28, 1945.

following year in November 1975. He contacted me when my husband Art and I were living in Colorado perhaps because his wife, Ione, had family in nearby Longmont. Jack and Ione visited us in Fort Collins, and Jack kindly brought a couple lovely dishes that had been in the Holasek family that he thought I would like.

Mother's father Stanley Svec was the only grandparent that I remember. Grandpa Svec continued to live in the same house at 105 9th Avenue North after his wife died and their children had married and moved away. He had the house remodeled so he could rent the downstairs and have his living quarters upstairs. A stairway in the back of the house gave him a separate entrance to his apartment. I remember climbing those steps many times when our family visited him.

The first room we entered was his living room with comfortable chairs and his large roll top desk which intrigued me with its many little drawers where he kept pencils, pens, a magnifying glass, paper clips, and other writing supplies. He usually sat in his swivel chair by the desk while we visited. Grandpa Svec enjoyed working outside, especially tending his large rose garden on the side of the house. In the backyard, he had a goldfish pool that fascinated Dorothy and me as we watched the fish swim around.

Grandpa Svec often visited our family at our home. After retiring from the grocery store, he joined with a friend in the plumbing business and always helped us if we had problems with sinks, drains, or other plumbing issues. He brought Dorothy and me toys, and I eventually realized that he was responsible for the beautiful baskets that arrived on our front porch every Easter morning. He was a wonderful, jolly, and affectionate grandfather who loved his grandchildren. In 1949, Grandpa Svec had a stroke and had to go to a nursing home, where he passed away. I remember being surrounded by relatives at his funeral as they reminisced about his grocery store, his athleticism when young, and his beautiful rose garden.

Stanley Svec in his rose garden, c 1946.

Stanley Svec with Richard, Dorothy, and Janet.

Mother's youngest sister Gloria "Glo" and her husband Norman "Norm" came to visit and get eggs at least once a week. People said their marriage was made in heaven. Gloria had a marvelous smile and laugh and was always somewhat overweight due to her craving for chocolate, especially M&M's, which later contributed to her diabetes. She dressed fashionably and wore a perfume that had a mild but distinctive fragrance I will always remember. Aunt Gloria had a rag-mop-type dog that often came with them, and she would carry it around under her arm. Uncle Norman, tall and handsome, always had a sparkle in his eyes, gleaming white teeth, a slight mustache that he would wiggle for effect, and a joke for every occasion. Just seeing him made me smile. Kind, generous, and helpful, Norman was always there when needed. He had an auto parts business in Minneapolis that did very well. His mother, who maintained her posture and good looks until old age, worked for him. One story passed down was that Norman's beautiful teeth were due to being nursed by his mother until he was four years old.

Glo and Norm built a beautiful house in Minnetonka Mills in the 1940s. It had a separate screen porch about 200 feet from the house, on a bit of a hill. They had three children: Roger, Kay, and Patricia. Roger was just a year older than Dorothy, Kay was my age, and Patty was a year or two younger than me. I still remember going into their house for the first time. It seemed so big and had a living room a few steps down from the dining room and kitchen. Visits to their house were the best! They had swings and bars to play on by the screen house, and board games to play indoors. The atmosphere was always cheerful and happy.

Norman and Gloria (Svec) White celebrating their 50th wedding anniversary, 1983.

Once their children were grown, Glo and Norm sold their house and moved to an apartment in Hopkins. In 1975, they followed their dream. They left their apartment, leaving their few belongings with their children, and bought an RV to travel the

United States. Glo developed diabetes which affected her eyesight and worsened with age, and she passed away in 1989. Norman went to live in northern Minnesota where his son Roger and daughter-in-law Lorraine operated a resort. Uncle Norman passed away there in 1994. I will forever remember him with the mischievous look in his eyes, his ready smile, and the twitching mustache that always preceded a joke.

Mother and her sister Sylvia, who was three years younger, remained fairly close over the years. Sylvia began playing a half-size violin when young. After high school, she worked as a stenographer and continued to play the violin. A woman in Hopkins noticed her talent and offered to pay her way to Hamline University. There, she met Robert "Rob" Holliday, and they married in 1933. Rob began teaching at Hamline in 1938 and in 1942, he became the director of Hamline's well-known and admired a cappella choir. Sylvia continued her violin studies and later, held a seat with the St. Paul Chamber Orchestra for many years. They lived in St. Paul but came out to visit my parents occasionally. Daddy always seemed ill at ease during these visits, and while Rob and Sylvia never gave the impression of being superior, Daddy felt inwardly inferior to college-educated folk.

Mother adored Sylvia and always commented on how beautiful she was. She wore her hair swept up in the back, always dressed fashionably, and carried herself with a certain sophistication that never overshadowed the warmth of her personality. Charming would best describe her.

Sylvia (left) and Evelyn (right) at sister Gloria's 50th wedding anniversary, 1983.

Robert and Sylvia Holliday at sister Gloria's 50th wedding anniversary, 1983.

Sylvia and Rob had two sons, both talented artistically; Peter in visual arts and Kent who became an established pianist and professor at Virginia Tech University. In the 1970s, Mother and Sylvia met for lunch as often as possible. Mother, who had a financial bent, suggested that Sylvia take advantage of the high interest rates for the family's savings. The two women exchanged recipes, reminisced, and enjoyed each other's company. When Sylvia passed away in 1994, less than a month after her husband's death, Mother could not be consoled. She and Sylvia had become very close over the last several years of Sylvia's life. Mother felt that life was so unfair, and that she should have gone first being the oldest sister.

Card playing, especially 500 and sometimes euchre, brought friends and family together. When Dorothy went on Hamline's Washington Semester program in the spring of 1960, she and Bob

Family gathering after Sylvia's memorial service, left to right: Evelyn, Peter Holliday, Kent Holliday, Cheryl Holliday Galloway (Kent's daughter), Kay White Hunke (Gloria and Norman White's daughter), April 1994.

Barrett were already engaged. Dorothy had applied and scheduled this before the engagement, and she was not going to cancel it now that she was engaged. Washington Semester gave her an opportunity to study in the D.C. area for one semester and connect with political figures. She would get credit at Hamline University for courses she took.

At this time, Bob was finishing his last semester at Hamline University and missed Dorothy so much that he would come to our house almost every Saturday night to play 500 with us. That was our favorite card game. Mother and Bob would be partners against Daddy and me. Mother always served pie and *kolach* midway through the evening. Daddy enjoyed playing cards, and these Saturday nights were among the few times that I saw him truly happy. I still remember him sitting with a smirk on his face as Bob got the bid with eight hearts. The play proceeded and with two plays left, Daddy would rise from his chair and throw a trump card on Bob's play with a "take that!" then, "and this!" as he played the highest card left to be played in hearts, which kept Bob from making his bid. Bob took being set in stride, and we all had a good laugh.

My parents also enjoyed playing 500 with Frank and Mary Neumeister who lived about a half mile down the road. Mary enjoyed talking and always seemed to be smiling, while Frank sat quietly, nodding in agreement. They came in the winter months, and Mother always served blueberry pie and *kolach* when they took a break from playing cards. My parents returned the visit a few weeks later, and the couples went back and forth to each other's homes during the winter when there was little or no work to be done outside.

The Neumeisters were part of the larger Czech community in the Hopkins-Eden Prairie area. In 1904, at the age of 17, Frank J. Neumeister came from Oldris Cechy, Bohemia, with his friend Joseph Sidla. Frank first worked on the farm of Edward Bren, another Czech farmer, and next at the Minneapolis Threshing Machine Company in Hopkins. He saved to buy 20 acres of land from Frank Stodola on Baker Road where he built his own home in 1911 and married Mary Kuchera in November of that year. Mary was born in the United States, but her parents had emigrated to the United States from Bohemia. Frank and Mary planted an enormous field of raspberries in addition to having farm animals. Both were hard-working Czechs who kept their language but learned English over the years, Frank keeping his distinct accent.

Frank was the quieter of the two and was often seen plowing in the field with his single horse. When it was not berry season, Mary would go to town to shop. Frank would leave the horse in the middle of the field to take Mary to the bus at the Glen Lake Sanatorium or to Hopkins. The horse never moved and remained in the field swishing its tail at flies, waiting for Frank to return to continue plowing. Neighbors would go by and just smile seeing the horse standing alone, knowing that Mary had decided to go to town.

They raised two sons, Frank, Jr., who died at 18, and Charles "Charley," who became a well-known surgeon in the Minneapolis area. After high school, Charley worked at the Northrup King Seed Company for a few years to save money for college, and then attended the University of Minnesota where he earned his medical degree.

Janet and Art's wedding reception, left to right: Mabel Reuter, Mrs. and Mr. Neumeister, George Reuter, unidentified person, 1967.

Charley's reputation grew in the medical community as a leading Minneapolis proctologist and surgeon. He never forgot his roots and returned often to visit his parents after making his home in Edina with his wife Eunice Zradzil. I remember Mother talking about people who went to see Charley with their medical problems. Always a kind and caring person, he helped anyone needing his medical advice and often attracted people from the Hopkins area. He died suddenly, much too young, at the age of 62 on January 7, 1979. His mother Mary had had a stroke in January 1973 and preceded him in death in 1974 at the age of 82. Frank sold the farm in 1977 with the understanding that he could continue to live there as long as he wished. Eventually, he needed to go into a nursing home. His last years passed slowly for him, as his wife and sons had all preceded him in death. Only his daughter-in-law Eunice survived him. Dorothy visited Frank in those last years and was saddened by his loneliness and the sense that he was just waiting to die. He passed away in December 1982 at the age of 94. The last time I saw Mary and Frank was in 1967 when they came to Art's and my wedding and gave us a pair of pillowcases which Mary had beautifully embroidered and crocheted at the ends. I still have them and use them on end tables so I can see Mary's handiwork and recall memories of dear friends.

My parents had a telephone for a year or two, but the lines ran through the woods and winds frequently knocked them down, so the phone company discontinued the service. For years, we went to our neighbors Winfred and Dell Eckert when we had to use a phone. We took a shortcut through the woods on a path by the garden and up a hill, picking mayflowers and violets that covered the ground along the way. We crawled through a hole in a fence, followed a path through a wooded area, and came out by the Eckert's house.

They always greeted us warmly and let us use their telephone. They had two sons, Jim, the same age as Dorothy, and Royal, several years older. Mr. Eckert often took us swimming in Bryant Lake in the summer. He would let us paddle around in the shallow water and watched us from the dock. He was such a kind, wonderful neighbor. He died in 1966, and Mrs. Eckert continued to live in their house until she sold it in 1976. Eventually, we got our own phone, but not until the 1950s, and then it had a party line so you never knew who listened to your conversations.

Royal Eckert standing behind, left to right: Jim Eckert, Janet, Dorothy, c. 1946.

We occasionally saw other neighbors such as Violet and Emil Kroger who lived across the road on the corner. They both worked in Minneapolis, married late in life, and never had any children. We didn't socialize with them but would see them outside and chat with them when walking home from the sanatorium. Sometimes, they invited us in for a cool drink in the summer. Every Christmas, Violet would bring us a Christmas present, usually candy or something special to eat. I still have a metal candy box from her which I have used for buttons. When the Krogers moved, the Kaeffer family bought their house. Mrs. Kaeffer was a fantastic cook, excelling in desserts, like her scrumptious meringue pie. She visited us occasionally and always brought one of her desserts. The Kaeffers had to vacate the house in the spring of 1977 for construction on County Road 62.

Dorothy and Janet with neighbor Mrs. Emil Kroger before going to school, 1947.

Dr. Lindquist became a family friend over the years. His wife had died some years before we knew him. He walked with a decided limp and used a cane, but that didn't stop him from driving and getting around. He and his wife never had any children, and I believe he thought of me as the daughter he never had. When I had chiropractor treatments, Mother would come and sit to the side, visiting with him for the 20-minute session. Patients wore white hospital-type gowns and would lie on a bed-like couch similar to those we see in a doctor's office today.

When I got older and went to appointments alone, he took his receptionist Ada Grenier and me to dinner at the Leamington Hotel in Minneapolis. He would then drive me home. When I was in high school, he asked if I needed any dresses and took me to Dayton's to buy a lovely, yellow, Easter dress. Another time, he took me to Dayton's and bought me a beautiful blue coat. I wore it for years and took it to Ireland with me when Art and I went in 1969. I think he enjoyed these outings and was probably quite lonely. We continued to be in contact over the years, and the last time I saw him was when he came to Art's and my wedding with his receptionist.

In the last several years that Mother lived in Minnesota, Rosie (Holasek) Pavelka and Mother became close friends. They had known each other for years, as Rosie was part of the extended Holasek family. They saw each other at weddings and funerals or at chance encounters in the grocery store. Rosie lived in Eden Prairie where she and her husband Alfred Pavelka built a house. They had a huge vegetable garden and Rosie loved working outside. I do not

Dr. Oscar Lindquist and receptionist Ada Grenier in their office waiting room, Minneapolis, 1950s.

know what brought Rosie and my mother together into their close friendship, perhaps it was Rosie's compassion and generosity. But when Daddy's health declined in the 1990s, Rosie often stopped to visit my parents, bringing fresh vegetables from her garden. Often, she came on Sundays on her way to or from attending the Faith Presbyterian Church located less than a mile from my parents' house. Rosie was a kind person with an exuberant personality. Her visits gave my parents a bit of relief and happiness during a difficult time.

After Daddy went into the nursing home, Rosie took Mother to lunch as a way to give her a change in scenery. Mother enjoyed these outings and the chance to talk with someone about gardening, cooking, and life in general. They both knew many of the same people, having a common Czech background and would reminisce about their friends and family. Rosie visited Mother almost weekly, always bringing her fresh vegetables or baked goods. As Mother said, "We enjoyed each other's company as there weren't many of us our age left!" When Mother moved to Colorado, Rosie was the person Mother said she would miss the most. They kept in touch for a few years through letters and in one that Rosie had written to Mother, Rosie mentioned how much she missed their Sunday visits.

Evelyn (left) and Rosie (Holasek) Pavelka (right) enjoying lunch together, 1995.

17. THE HOLASEK HOUSE

The following is a description of the house where Dorothy and I grew up. Some of the information repeats earlier pages but is integral to describing the house.

The Holasek house at 6233 Baker Road was built on land that was part of the acreage Joseph Holasek acquired over the years and later parceled out to his children for their farms. Records are unclear as to the date, but Steve Holasek—probably with help from his brothers Winslow and John—built the house around 1890 with Chaska bricks. Famous for their cream color and high clay content found in the Chaska, Minnesota, area, the bricks came from one of several brickyards in Chaska. The Holasek house had two stories and a basement with a cement floor. The basement could be entered from either the outside or an inside stairway.

A cement stairway on the east side of the house led to an entrance to the basement, accessed by raising a large, flat, wooden door that could be propped up with a metal rod. The stairway ended in a 15-foot-long cement passageway that we called the cellarway, which stayed cool year round and was downright cold in the winter. It acted as a refrigerator to cool meat after butchering, freshly made sausage, and crocks of sauerkraut.

The cellarway led to a door into the basement itself. The large, open space that made up most of the basement housed the

Evelyn in front of Holasek house on 6233 Baker Road, Hopkins, c. 1950s.

wood-burning furnace with its pipes leading to upstairs vents. In the winter, Daddy kept a fire going day and night, feeding it wood, from the pile stacked next to the furnace. He saved the biggest pieces to add at night to create as much heat as possible all night long. That was the last thing he did before going to bed. Sometimes, I went down to the basement with him to watch. He opened the latch on the big, black iron, furnace door. I could see the blazing fire inside or the nest of coals and feel the heat. He would toss a huge chunk of wood onto the coals and quickly shut the furnace door. The wood had been brought into the basement in the fall and piled next to the furnace.

The stack would be replenished several times during the winter from woodpiles outside. This large room also housed the Amana freezer.

Eventually, an oil burning furnace replaced the big wood-burning monster. This opened up the basement, so Mother hung clotheslines to dry clothes inside during the winter instead of outside. Thus, an end came to the stiff, frozen sheets, towels, and clothing that were first hung outside then brought inside to dry by heat registers throughout the house. But the end also came to the wonderful, fresh smell of clothes partially dried outdoors.

The clothes washing machine and two laundry sinks sat in a small room in the southeast corner of the basement. The washing machine was a square, metal tub with an agitator. Once washed, Mother hand-fed the clothes through the attached wringer, letting them fall into a large wicker basket lined with paper. I loved to stand and watch the flattened clothes come through the wringer. In the summer, she hung them outside on the slight hill south of the house. The trees there supported the clotheslines and she put "clothes poles" in the middle of the line to keep the line from sagging. Daddy made these poles from tree branches that had a Y at the end which could support the clothesline. I enjoyed helping hang the clothes. Once we hung them, we left the basket outside until it was time to gather the dry clothes and bring them inside, often leaving the basket temporarily in the kitchen. One evening, a garter snake startled us as it tried to get across the slippery kitchen floor! Where did it come from? It probably crawled into the newspapers lining the clothes basket while the basket was outside, and then came inside with the clothes.

We quickly swept it into a large paper bag and carried it back outside!

At the entry to this basement laundry room sat what we called the wood box and next to it stacks of wood. When Mother needed wood for the kitchen stove, she filled the wood box in the basement. She went up to the kitchen and cranked the woodbox via an attached rope, bringing it into the kitchen pantry, right next to the wood-burning stove. It was a rather clever system to keep the kitchen supplied with wood. Also, tucked into a corner of the basement laundry room was a toilet, the only one in the house besides one in a second-floor bedroom. I don't know if the toilets were put in when the house was built. Perhaps later which would explain the three-hole outhouse a distance from the barn.

We called the small room in the southwest corner of the basement the vegetable room. Here, shelves held all the Ball and Kerr jars of fruits and vegetables that Mother had canned during the summer. I never knew why they were called canned, because they were in glass jars! Tomatoes, beets, corn, pears, peaches, green beans, pickles, and much more filled the shelves in rows. These provided wonderful meals throughout the year and represented hours of work with Mother standing over the boiling kettle and gently lifting out the jars after the requisite cooking time. The room also held the large Red Wing crocks of carrots as well as squash and bags of onions and potatoes, which lasted all winter.

Perhaps the most important function of this room came during Minnesota's fierce thunder and lightning storms. As the storm grew in intensity, we rushed down the inside basement steps and huddled in a corner for protection from potential tornadoes. Because of its location, it was deemed to be the safest spot in the house. The wind could be heard whistling outside, and flashes of lightning could be seen through the one tiny window in the room. When the storm blew over, we carefully made our way up the steps which led to the main floor dining room.

The main or ground floor of the house had two entrances. Virtually everyone used the back entrance with its four large cement steps leading to a porch and into the kitchen. We left snow boots and muddy shoes on the porch, but otherwise we wore our shoes in the house. The porch had a window into the kitchen, and Mother had a table on the porch right next to the window. She could just open the window and put anything that she wanted to keep cold on the table. In the winter, this functioned as a refrigerator, but she had to be careful, because in 20-below weather, foods would freeze there. The porch had a screen door which let in cool breezes, making it a very comfortable spot to shell peas, tip green beans, and prepare other garden produce during hot summer days.

The kitchen was rectangular in shape, with the north and south walls about one third the length of the east and west walls. Upon entering the kitchen through a beautiful, carved wooden door, the north wall to the left had hooks for coats and jackets. This was something of an eyesore, but it was the design of the kitchen when originally built. Cupboards and storage areas for dishes and cooking utensils covered half of the east wall. It was here that Mother kept her treasured stainless-steel mixing bowls and frying pans. She loved stainless steel, and I still use many of her bowls and saucepans. Next came a cabinet in front of a window looking to the east, a sink, and then a refrigerator in the corner. The cabinet had a built-in bread board which pulled out. Here, Mother rolled pie crusts and made countless batches of *kolach*. A large drawer in the cabinet had a flour bin with a scoop and a place for sugar.

The house had no sink other than the one in the upstairs bathroom, so when Daddy came in from chores, he had to use the kitchen sink to wash up. He pulled out a basin from under the sink and thoroughly washed his hands and face. At the same time, Mother would be making dinner or supper and often needed the sink but had to wait for Daddy to finish.

A window looked out to the south and a big, black wood stove occupied the corner and part of the west wall of the kitchen. The stove pipes carrying the heat were near the ceiling on the west wall, and I remember Mother watching them so they wouldn't start turning red, indicating too hot a fire in the stove. If they got too hot, they could cause the house to catch on fire. Once, when they started to turn color, Mother quickly put wet towels on them so they would cool down. Later, an electric stove replaced the wood stove. Next to the stove, a door opened to the pantry and wood box. Along the wall, Mother placed a chair where she put the milk pasteurizer and additional chairs for the occasional visitor. At the end of the wall, Daddy built a shelf for the radio. The wall ended with an archway going into the dining room.

The kitchen—being the warmest room in the house and the place where Mother spent most of her time—quickly became the center of the house. Dorothy and I had little school desks there where we drew, wrote, and colored. When visitors came, they usually stayed in the kitchen where Mother would be baking or preparing meals. We ate breakfast and usually lunch at the kitchen table, always covered with a tablecloth which Mother made. The wooden table had a porcelain top with four matching wooden chairs. Daddy always sat at the north end of the table and Mother opposite him, while Dorothy and I sat on either side. I remember it as a warm and welcoming room painted a pale yellow.

Through the archway on the west side of the kitchen, one entered the dining room with its handsome, round wooden table dominating the center. If the table could talk, it would have many a story to tell in its nearly 50 years of service. It had four leaves which stretched the table so far that it had to sit diagonally in the room to feed the threshing crew in the fall. Every evening, our family of four sat around the table for the evening meal. The best evenings came when family and relatives gathered round the table to play 500, euchre, and other card games.

A buffet or sideboard occupied the east side of the dining room, while two beautiful wood-framed windows dominated the north wall. Mother loved the ruffled priscilla curtains which were popular then and draped them on both windows. Between the windows, hung an antique cuckoo clock that came from Mother's parents' house. A cuckoo bird came out of a little door near the top every hour. I liked to wind the clock by pulling the two weights on chains hanging from the bottom.

Dorothy at her wedding shower in Holasek house. Note buffet and wooden window frame with priscilla curtains, 1960.

In the northwest corner of the dining room, a door opened to the wooden steps leading to the basement. On the west wall, an archway opened to a hallway that led to the stairway going upstairs. Mother had her treadle sewing machine in the hallway and a dresser with a three-way mirror that we all used to fix our hair. A wooden door at the end of the hall opened onto a porch which was enclosed with many windows but not heated, so we only used it in the summer. It had a couch, a few chairs, and an old hand crank phonograph which worked until Dorothy and I wanted to see what happened if we cranked it 100 times. We found out... On the 100th turn of the crank, it went "BOOM" and never worked again! A flimsy screen door led outside and constituted the front entrance to our house. While very few people used this entrance, I do remember that the Easter bunny left Dorothy and me baskets there when we were small. Often our Grandpa Svec visited on Easter morning, and we never connected the two events!

The south side of the dining room had a double archway that opened into the living room. A tall, upright piano—where both Dorothy and I learned to play—dominated this room on the east wall. A couch occupied the south wall and in the southwest corner, we put our first television in December 1950, a small black and white Philco. A large brown, tattered rocking chair sat in the northwest corner next to a heat register, making it a prized spot where Daddy sat during winter evenings reading the newspaper. Often, he would take his glasses off and put them on the floor by the rocking chair. I liked to stand by the heat register and look at the paper with him. Once, as I was getting closer to the heat register, I heard a crunch. I had stepped on his glasses. He reached down and picked them up, calmly saying, "That's why we should always look where we step." He carefully carried them into the kitchen and no more was said about it, but I felt terrible.

When Dorothy and I were young, the family bedroom was in the room west of the living room; tan draperies, trimmed in brown, separated the two rooms. The wood furnace simply did not give off enough heat to make the upstairs warm enough for sleeping when we were small. I would have terrible coughing fits at night and, many a night, Mother slept on the couch in the living room, holding my hand in the crib next to her. Mother tried everything to stop my coughing, from having me lie on my stomach over a pillow to fixing me warm, honey-lemon drinks. Once Dorothy and I were older, we all slept upstairs year round. Flannel sheets and several warm blankets made the cooler upstairs temperatures tolerable. My parents converted the downstairs bedroom into an additional living room with comfortable chairs, sofa, end tables, lamps, and Dorothy's phonograph.

The beautiful wooden stairway with its hand-carved spindles led to the second floor. It began with a one-step landing, went up 10 steps to another landing, turned a corner, and went up four more steps. Immediately to the right was a beautiful handmade cupboard with vertical doors opening onto shelves. Here, Mother kept some seasonal clothes, spare blankets, her sewing supplies, and fabric. Below, four drawers provided space where she kept sheets, towels, and linens. This cupboard, plus all the identical wooden door frames, are a testimony to Steve Holasek's craftsmanship.

To the left of the stairs, a hall ran the length of the top floor. From the stairs, a bit to the right, was the best room. It had windows to the west and south and a large walk-in closet. This was Dorothy's room with a bed, dresser, desk, and other smaller pieces of furniture. At some point in the 1950s, we painted all the rooms upstairs, and she chose peach for her room.

The room next to it had southern windows letting in warmth

Holasek house stairway (left), top of stairs entering second floor (right).

and light and making it, I think, the most pleasant room. This was my room. Again, a bed, desk, dresser, and small table filled the space. I loved my desk which we found at a second-hand store in Hopkins. It had a drop-down writing area with a shelf underneath for books. My room had a small walk-in closet with a wonderful cupboard with shelves where I kept scrapbooks and things I collected over time. I helped paint the room a warm yellow.

Mother and Daddy's room was at the end of the hall, a corner room where the bathroom was also located. A heavy curtain divided the room in half, separating the toilet, sink, and bathtub from the rest of the room. It was above the kitchen, and a vent which could be opened and closed let in warm air from the kitchen. The other portion of the room had a bed, end table, lamp, and dresser. Daddy chose to paint this room chartreuse, which we all found amusing. It was a popular color at the time, but we never thought he would choose something so bright.

A trapdoor in the ceiling of the bedroom closet led to the attic. It had to be lifted off and slid onto the attic floor. The attic was hot and stuffy, but a treasure land for Dorothy and me when we were small. It had all sorts of old books, clothes, two trunks, and items Mother brought from her parents' house when they passed away. It even had the old raspberry carriers used by berry pickers in the 1920s! At some point, Mother cleaned it all out, but that was after Dorothy and I had left for college.

The last and smallest room was across the hall from my room, on the north side, and unsurprisingly called the north room. We used it as storage for seasonal clothes, rarely worn clothes, and the cedar chest. We always kept its door closed and heat register turned off.

Our house was encircled by a driveway of crushed rock. The iron fence with cement posts that enclosed it made it a landmark at the very edge of Eden Prairie Township. The last big event in the Holasek house was Art's and my wedding reception on June 10, 1967. I remember in the late afternoon of that day, Daddy, Art, and I walked up and across the hill, less than a quarter of a mile to the south, to see the foundation of their new house, known as the pink house.

Changes came quickly to the once rural, agricultural Eden Prairie. Interstate 494 cut through the east side of my parents' farm with State Highway 62 being built on the northern border of their land to link up with Interstate 494. In 1960, the state of Minnesota

Holasek house with pump and tool shed (center), barn (left).

condemned land where my family had grown strawberries and where the cows pastured over the years for the Interstate. This was the beginning of a piecemeal breakup of the farm as homes and condominiums replaced alfalfa, corn, and grain fields over the next 30 years.

In early 1967, my parents had sold land which included the house and barn to Standard Oil Company, with plans to move to their new home in the fall. Mother did most of the planning and packing for the move and said it all went smoothly, except when a pickup truck hauling an old family dresser with a wooden arch over its top caught on a low hanging branch as the truck continued on. The old dresser was left swinging, as if saying goodbye to its home of over 70 years!

In 1977, Arteka Inc., a landscape business, bought the homesite, finding the location near State Highway 62 and Interstate 494 particularly attractive. They used the Holasek house as an office building. They remodeled it, turning bedrooms and closets into offices and installing computers and copiers. This removed the house from ever being considered for the National Register of Historical Buildings. When Arteka sold the site to Normandale Tennis Club, Arteka kept possession of the building but had to move it. The house was placed on steel girders and on June 17, 1986, it was moved one-half mile further north to Minnetonka Township. Arteka soon

Holasek house being moved, June 17, 1986. Eden Prairie News, January 28, 1987, photo by Mark Weber, Eden Prairie House - Historical Society. Courtesy of Thomas Achartz.

decided to build a new office building and offered the Holasek house to the city of Eden Prairie for one dollar. After considerable debate, the Eden Prairie City Council turned down the offer in February 1987.

Arteka donated the house to Camp Eden Wood, an Eden Prairie retreat center run by ARC (a nonprofit providing advocacy and support for people with disabilities) just inside Eden Prairie Township. The house was moved back into Eden Prairie, about a half mile to the southwest of where it had been in Minnetonka. It became living quarters for the caretaker and held the administrative offices. In 1995, Friendship Ventures (a non-profit offering recreational activities for people with disabilities) bought Camp Eden Wood and continued to use the Holasek house as office space.

In the summer of 2010, Dorothy and I visited our house at Camp Eden Wood where one of the staff members showed us around. We saw the beautiful wood cabinets that Steve Holasek had built, and the woodwork throughout the house looked amazing for its age. The house functioned as a dormitory for staff. In the next decade, Camp Eden Wood built new housing, and the Holasek house was vacated. The need for complete renovation of the house was prohibitive from a cost standpoint.

I last saw the house in October 2022, when my cousin Annette and I visited thanks to True Friends' CEO John LeBlanc who opened the house and walked us through. It looked lonely and forlorn, sitting at a distance from the rest of the camp buildings, in an open space. Some of the wood frames around windows, solid wooden doors, and the inside wooden staircase with its spindles that

Janet and Dorothy in front of Holasek house at Camp Eden Wood, 2010.

Dorothy and I dusted over 70 years ago, still remain. The metal heat vents and brass doorknobs inside harken back to its heyday. For over 100 years, the Chaska brick has withstood countless snowstorms, wind, and hailstorms. Perhaps, some of the interior woodwork can be salvaged and even repurposed. Hopefully, this chapter preserves memories of the three generations that called the Holasek house home.

Janet and cousin Annette (Makousky) Greer in Annette's condo, Minnetonka, Minnesota, 2022.

18. THE HOLASEK BARN

The sight of a large red barn with an attached or nearby silo speaks to the Midwest's immigrant and family farm history. These barns rose in the late 19th and early 20th century; few if any remain in use today. Instead, the family farm has been replaced by large, mechanized dairy farms with herds of over 100 dairy cows instead of the 20 to 30 on a family farm. The early barns had many similarities: a hayloft, large storage areas, horse stalls, stanchions for cows, mangers for hay and silage, and water tanks. They sat on a concrete foundation with the lower level leading to a fenced-in cow yard. Below is a look inside the Holasek barn, which is representative of the red barns dotting the Minnesota landscape.

The barn had three stories. The top story was the hay mow or hayloft where loose hay was stored. Using the pulley system described in Chapter 9, the hay entered the hayloft through the giant door on the north side of the barn. Later in the day, Daddy climbed into the hayloft on an inside wooden ladder and used a pitchfork to spread the bunches of hay evenly over the floor of the loft. After this hot and exhausting job, he came into the house ready for several glasses of ice-cold lemonade that Mother had ready. When it was time to feed the cows, Daddy climbed into the hayloft and tossed hay to the barn's main level, then through a trap door in the floor, and down to the cows' mangers on the level below. He would leave some hay on the main floor to feed the horses.

Sometimes, a hired man chose to sleep in the hayloft on hot summer days. During the Depression, wandering men seeking shelter would bed down in the hayloft, and then leave in the early morning hours, or stay and ask for work.

The main level of the barn served many functions. One entered through two huge doors on the north side below the hayloft door. Immediately to the left were three horse stalls. The first stall held harnesses for the horses, hoes, shovels, rakes, and other garden implements. The two work horses occupied the next two stalls which had loose straw on the floor for bedding. In front of the horses, feeding bins held their oats and hay. Next came a walkway on the left which led to a huge open area for hay tossed from the loft, the storage of straw bales, and miscellaneous farm tools and equipment.

Across from the horse stalls, on the right, was a chicken coop for young chicks. Next to the chickens and across from the walkway sat the hand crank corn sheller where Mother used to shell corn for the chickens. The large area in the middle, between the horse stalls and chickens, was where Daddy parked the tractor, usually in the winter when not in use.

Two big swinging doors separated this room from a similar room on the south side which was often empty, except in the winter when Daddy parked the truck there. Immediately to the left of the swinging doors were steps leading to the barn's lower level. Lighting was not very good there, and one had to be careful going down the steps. Across from the steps and along the wall was a water faucet and water tank where Daddy led the horses several times a day for water. Along the wall, two doors opened into smaller rooms, each also having a door to the outside.

The room on the southwest corner was called the bunk. It held a jumble of miscellaneous farm items from hoes to raspberry and strawberry carriers and was the storage area for new strawberry and raspberry crates. It could be entered from either inside the barn or from a door on the outside. The other room, next to the water tank, was the milkhouse which held the Surge tank filled with cold water, where Daddy put the filled milk cans. The room also had a huge sink where he washed the Surge milkers and put them on an adjacent drying rack. A floor drain allowed for the escape of dirty water. A door led to the outside, where the milkman entered every morning to pick up the filled milk cans from the water tank. At night, Daddy always left a saucer with milk outside the door for the barn cats. Two large doors on the barn's south side, like those on the north side, gave access to this area as well as to the bunk and milkhouse from the inside.

On the south side of the barn, to the right of the two large doors, was the garage for the car. A small concrete driveway led into the garage, which was fine when cars were small, but as cars increased in size, it was a tight fit! I never tried to put the green 1953 Chevrolet in the garage and left that for Daddy to do.

Next to the garage was a gigantic sliding door. A similar door was across from it on the north side. I remember a couple of times when one of the wheels keeping the door in place came off the track. Mother and Daddy had a difficult time lifting the door ever so

Holasek barn with pump and tool shed, note barn door leading to room where milk was cooled.

Remodeled Holasek barn with large sliding door (right), the stairway and openings on south side did not exist on original barn, 1966.

slightly to get it back on track. These doors led to the large part of the barn used for storage and where hay was tossed down from the hayloft as described earlier.

Outside the sliding door on the south side of the barn was a large concrete drainage area. I am not sure what its purpose was when built. At one time, a tree must have been nearby, because I remember a stump about 24 inches high where Mother used to kill chickens. She put the chicken's head on the stump and, with one quick blow of her axe on the chicken's neck, the head fell off. She held the chicken by the feet while it still fluttered, spraying blood around, until it stopped moving, and then the dressing process began. The iron picket fence surrounding the house began here with a gate that led to the cow yard which also was surrounded by the fence. Next to the gate was the smokehouse, not used in my memory, and about 100 feet up a slight hill, was a three-seater outhouse. I imagine it had been used in the past, but I have no recollection of it ever being used.

Now, back to the barn. The lower level could be entered from the outside through the cow yard or from the inside, down the concrete steps on the main level. Entering, going down these steps, to the right was a chicken coop which held laying hens. To the left of the steps were two rows of cow stanchions with mangers in front for silage and hay. Later, after the barn's remodeling, chickens occupied this area.

Farther to the left, inside the barn on the lower level, was the entrance to the base of the silo from the inside of the barn. The silo was added to the barn in 1938. A ladder led to the top of the silo with doorways cut into the silo all the way to the top to allow entrance. When the silo was full, either Mother or Daddy climbed the ladder and entered the silo at the silage level and tossed the silage down. They carried it in buckets to the mangers in front of the cows.

On the east end of the barn were the two cow doors through which the cows entered and exited the barn into the cow yard. Straight ahead and just beyond the cow yard was the pig pen where my parents had several pigs that rooted around in a fenced area. By about the early 1950s, we stopped raising pigs for meat, and instead bought pork in the grocery store. About 200 feet beyond the pig pen was a pond which froze in the winter. Daddy would shovel off the snow so Dorothy and I could go ice-skating.

To the left of the barn and through a gate, was the granary with a huge bin for oats. Attached to the granary, but with horizontal strips of wood spaced about eight inches apart, was the corn crib. It was raised about a foot off the ground to keep out mice and other rodents.

Farm machinery was kept on a slight hill to the northwest of the barn and under a row of trees. This area led to the perimeter of the iron picket fence, with a gate opening into the garden. Just before the gate were two giant haystacks where my parents put extra hay that did not fit in the hayloft.

It is fascinating to look at income tax returns in the 1940s and 1950s, because they give the dates for the construction of farm buildings and major farm purchases for purposes of depreciation. If

Corn crib (left), north side of barn with door at top which swung down for putting hay in hayloft.

not for the tax returns, these dates would be unattainable. For example, the barn cost $4,400 to build. It was depreciated over 25 years, and each year my parents could claim $176 for it on their farm expenses. The silo was built in 1938 for $600 and depreciated over 25 years as well. Every year, my parents could claim $24 for it on their farm expenses. Smaller items like harnesses, horses, the milk cooler, and tractor were also depreciated over time, even though the farmer had to pay the full amount up front.

I do not know how long the barn remained after the farm was sold. At some point, I remember hearing that it had been remodeled to host dances. The hayloft and the open areas below would have been great for square dancing. Eventually, the barn was torn down and the whole area including the cow yard was scraped for future construction of a health club.

19. EPILOGUE

Mother and Daddy moved into the pink house in the fall of 1967. The ranch-style house was much more comfortable and convenient than the old house. Its double garage and entrance faced west. On entering, a hall led to three bedrooms and two baths on the left. Straight ahead from the entrance was the living room with a dining room to the right connected to a lovely kitchen which had a window facing Baker Road. The walkout basement had a living area with a fireplace and a garage for Daddy's tractor. The back of the house faced a largely untouched wooded area where raccoons and other wildlife lived. The grassy area in front of the house had several tall trees where Daddy hung the swing from the yard of the old house. He also hung a swing on a nearby tree for the grandchildren.

Driveway leading to Holasek's pink house with raspberry patch on left.

My mother and father lived in the pink house at 6375 Pinnacle Drive from 1967 until they sold the land it was on in 1989. These were their Golden Years. Dorothy lived in North Mankato and visited them with her two children at least once a month. Art and I came from Colorado every summer for several years with our three children. On December 12, 1974, children and grandchildren gathered to celebrate our parents' 50th wedding anniversary.

Throughout the 1970s and 1980s, my parents enjoyed watching their grandchildren grow up. On many occasions, when Dorothy needed to go to the University of Minnesota in Minneapolis, she left Annie and Geoffrey with Mother and Daddy. They gathered to celebrate birthdays and the Christmas holidays. In the summers, when Art and I came with our children, we made sure the cousins had time to play together. One of their favorite activities was riding the old red wagon down a hill filled with stumps and branches as I looked on in horror. They insisted on bringing the wagon to my parents' next house to continue their joyrides!

Mother and Daddy continued to have small patches of raspberries and strawberries. Mother had a vegetable garden and still froze berries and vegetables for the winter. Neighbors and friends stopped by to visit, and Mother made sure they left with some of her garden produce. She now had time to socialize with neighbors. They exchanged recipes, baked goods, and she even babysat for one of the mothers. Daddy busied himself cutting the lawn with a tractor-driven mower, tending the berries, and helping with hoeing in the garden. They both still enjoyed working outside. They took special pride in a ring of flowers they grew in front of the house which needed frequent watering.

Richard and Evelyn celebrating their 50th wedding anniversary, 1974.

Celebrating 50th wedding anniversary with family, left to right: Annie Barrett, Geoffrey Barrett, Dorothy Barrett, Richard, Janet Worrall holding Beth Worrall, Evelyn, Tim Worrall. Picture taken by Art Worrall.

Richard and Evelyn by ring of flowers at pink house.

Richard and Evelyn with grandchildren Geoffrey and Annie Barrett on swing by pink house.

Epilogue | 261

Richard and Evelyn with grandchildren Tom, Tim, and Beth Worrall on swing by pink house.

Lineup of grandchildren, left to right: Geoffrey, Tim, Beth, Annie, Tom.

Richard and Evelyn opening presents with grandchildren Geoffrey and Annie.

Evelyn with grandchildren Geoffrey and Annie at Christmas.

Evelyn with grandchildren Tom (in arms), Tim, and Beth.

Richard on tractor with grandchildren Tim and Beth.

Evelyn watering her garden at pink house with granddaughter Beth watching, 1988

Evelyn and Janet holding their raspberry carriers by raspberry patch.

In 1989, a health club bought the nearly five acres surrounding the pink house for tennis courts and a parking lot. The pink house was moved to an unknown location and the site is now overgrown with trees and underbrush with no indication that a house was ever there.

That same year, my parents moved to a ranch-style house a few miles away on Excelsior Boulevard known as the green house. The back of the house faced a wooded area—much like the area in the back of the pink house—keeping them in touch with nature. The living room looked out on Excelsior Boulevard, the dining room and small kitchen were in the back, and two bedrooms were off to the side. For the first time in their lives, my parents would have no garden or raspberry or strawberry patch. Mother still had house plants and rescued a dying African violet plant from a hardware store. She nursed it back to health and gave me three leaves to root. I still have the three plants which have beautiful, ruffled, pink flowers, and I think of Mother every time I water them. She also gave her granddaughter Beth a small geranium plant that is still alive and has been the source of many new geraniums for our flower gardens.

The bus to Minneapolis stopped in front of their house which made Mother happy, as Daddy could no longer drive and she loved her trips into town. Sometimes, she took the bus into Hopkins to get medicine, groceries, or Kentucky Fried Chicken to bring home for dinner. At the age of 90, she still managed the steep steps on the bus but, within the next year, she became worried that when she got off the bus and crossed the road to the house, she would not make it if a car was coming around a bend in the road. At that point, she began using taxis.

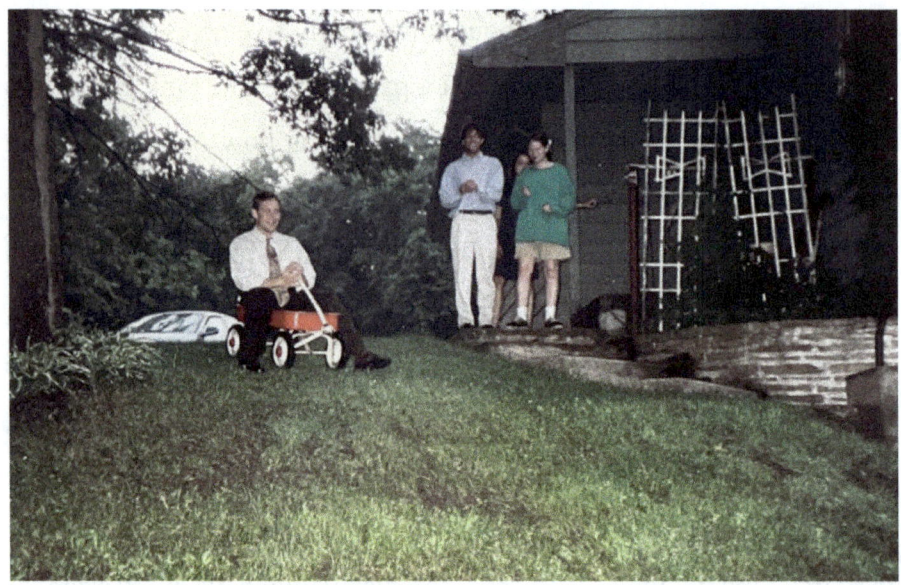

Tim in the infamous red wagon brought from the pink house. Tom, Annie, and Beth (standing behind) watching by green house.

Richard and Evelyn with grandchildren Geoffrey and Annie by green house.

Evelyn with Art Worrall by green house.

Evelyn in front of green house.

Daddy's health was declining and, by August 1994, Mother was no longer able to take care of him. For a couple of years, she had helped him get dressed, helped him to the bathroom, and steadied him as he walked. I saw a decline in her health, too. Her balance was affected, and she lost weight. Daddy had taken several falls but refused to let Mother call anyone to help him get up, so Mother struggled. Once, after four hours of his being on the floor after a fall, Mother insisted on calling the fire department to come and help.

Dorothy came from Mankato as often as possible to take Mother to get groceries and help with chores. A friend installed a railing into the basement and did other handyman chores to make the house safer.

Evelyn visiting Richard in the nursing home on their 70th wedding anniversary, December 12, 1994.

Daddy had always said, in no uncertain terms, that he would never go into a nursing home. I'll never forget when he returned home from the doctor one day to say, "Mama can no longer take care of me so I guess I need to go to a nursing home." Everyone was surprised yet relieved. Mother packed his clothes and moved him there in August 1994, with all his meds and other necessities. She visited him nearly every day. Our daughter Beth was working at the Mayo Clinic in Rochester at the time and often came up on weekends to take Mother grocery shopping. When in town, the grandchildren stopped to see him as Art and I did when we visited Minnesota. After 17 months in the nursing home, on a very cold, wintry day in January 1996, Daddy passed away peacefully in his sleep.

Dorothy and I encouraged Mother to move to Fort Collins, Colorado, where Art and I lived, rather than living alone with no close neighbors to help her if needed. We worried about her falling, as she now used a walker. She had been to Colorado several times to visit and began to mull the idea over in her mind. Both Dorothy and Beth lived nearly two hours away from her, but a move to Fort Collins meant she would be within minutes of where Art and I lived. Once she decided to move, she insisted on having her own apartment, because she did not want to burden us with her presence, not realizing that we would never think of her as a burden. Dorothy and I began preparations for the move while Mother started the process of selling her house.

In 1996, I went to stay with Mother over spring break, and Dorothy and I began packing and distributing household goods. That summer, I returned, and we cleared out the house. We made many trips to Goodwill and The Salvation Army with donated items and arranged for a moving company to take her furniture to Fort Collins. Mother successfully sold the house, and Dorothy and I were there for the closing. On July 24, 1996, Dorothy took Mother and me to the Minneapolis-St. Paul International Airport, and Mother said her final goodbye to Minnesota where she had lived her entire life. She loved to fly, and we had a beautiful flight to Colorado. Art picked us up at the new Denver International Airport, and we headed home to Fort Collins where Mother would spend the rest of her life.

Fortunately, a ground level apartment in a fourplex next door to where Art and I lived had become available in June, and we

Evelyn and Janet outside Evelyn's apartment in Fort Collins.

immediately signed a contract to rent it—a perfect arrangement. I saw Mother every day, and we had many shopping excursions. Dorothy and the grandchildren came to visit, and we were all together for Christmas in 1996. The next two years may have been the happiest of her life. She continued to read the daily paper and books I brought her. She did most of her own cooking and watched her favorite television shows.

Mother used a walker. But, after a few falls, she decided in May 1998 that it was time to go to a nearby assisted living facility. There, she participated in some of the social activities, especially the

Evelyn with granddaughter Annie (left) and Dorothy (right) in Evelyn's Fort Collins apartment, 1997.

Evelyn with grandson Geoffrey looking at album in Fort Collins, 1997.

spelling bees where she won the monthly trophy! She liked her own space and never complained about being lonely. She had meals with other residents in the dining hall and continued to do exercises learned at earlier physical therapy classes. I visited her nearly every day, Art came frequently, and our children stopped in to see her whenever they came to Fort Collins.

Mother had increasing problems with her hearing, and I think that limited her in being more active socially. At times, I could see her "sign out" when she just couldn't follow a conversation. Again and again, I urged her to get hearing aids, but her response always was, "Then people will think I am old!" This showed the stigma that people had toward hearing aids, which has fortunately disappeared. I have inherited this hearing deficit as have others in our family.

In February 1999, Mother was hospitalized with the flu and after several days in the hospital was moved to the Columbine nursing home. With her wry sense of humor, she said, "This is the last stop." But she continued to do her exercises to keep her remaining balance and ability to walk. She planned to make it to her 100th birthday. She almost made it but passed away on June 10, 2002, eight months short of turning 100. I had been sitting by her bed in the nursing home that day. Around 2:15 p.m., I told her I was going home briefly but would be back. She murmured that she heard me. Within 5 minutes of my getting home, which was a 10-minute drive, the phone rang. A woman from the nursing home said that Mother had passed. Had she waited for me to leave? We will never know.

Evelyn with her spelling bee trophy in the Columbine nursing home, Fort Collins, 2001.

In looking back, what does this memoir tell us about three generations of Czechs? The first generation, arriving in the 1850s, knew only hard work in order to survive. In the summers, they broke new ground and planted crops to harvest to get them through the winter. In the winters, they found jobs in Minneapolis to earn money for staples and to purchase government land. Czechs farmed lands adjacent to each other. Women tended their large families, often helping one another with a newborn or sitting together in the kitchen while knitting hats and mittens for the cold Minnesota winters. They needed the companionship of each other. About 80 percent of their contacts were with fellow Czechs, whether on nearby farms or with merchants in Hopkins. The Czech language prevailed. Marriage between Czech families happened more often than not.

Christmas with Evelyn in Columbine nursing home; Tim and wife Tamara standing; sitting left to right: Tom, Beth, Janet, 2000.

The second generation often had the good fortune of being given land by their parents as in the case of John and Steve Holasek and their siblings. Czechs in Hopkins, like Stanley Svec, were more entrepreneurial. They had a wider social network and participated in activities like Sokol, which honored their Czech heritage. That generation kept its language but also learned English. Women cooked authentic Czech food, passing on recipes to their children.

Like the previous generation, their social contacts remained predominantly within the Czech community.

The third generation, represented by my parents, lived during a transitional time in history. Their lives stretched from the first automobiles, to putting a man on the moon, to the computer age. They saw the destruction of two world wars separated by the Great Depression. For my parents, the family farm was their life. Nearby neighbors were Czech and, occasionally, you could hear the Czech language spoken. The Depression caused many farmers to go through foreclosures, but my parents managed to survive despite the drop in prices and the vagaries of weather. Horse-drawn farm equipment dominated until after World War II when tractors became available to farmers. Within the next five years, most work horses disappeared and, within the decade of the 1950s, the expense of mechanized farming would drive out the small family farm. Ethnicity as a bond had declined during this generation, and there was no expectation that children would have Czech spouses. Greater mobility for the children of this generation also meant widening their social network and meeting their future spouse outside the community.

Dorothy and I grew up during this generation. The question is, how were we shaped by the experience of being raised on the family farm? Above all was the strong work ethic instilled in us. There was no need for health and exercise clubs, as one got plenty of exercise doing family chores! My father never understood the popularity of spectator sports like football and baseball and saw them as a waste of time when you could be hoeing, making wood, or doing other field work.

Along with this work ethic came our frugal lifestyle. This may in part have been the result of our parents living through the Great Depression. Mother canned garden produce, meat came from butchered cows and pigs, and chickens were raised for eggs and, later, killed for dinner. Only a few staples needed to be purchased. Mother sewed many of our clothes and loved to go to church rummage sales where she would get great bargains. Garage sales have a similar attraction for me! I also sewed clothes for our children to save money, mainly when they were young. To this day, I cannot pass up a sale rack in a department store and rarely allow myself to pay full price for clothing.

Whenever Mother took a walk, she remarked on the beauty of a birch, maple, or oak tree. She loved the rustle of the leaves and liked nothing better than raking them in the fall as they fell from the trees. Dorothy and I gained our appreciation of nature from her. On our walks to get the cows from the pasture, we would identify the different kinds of trees and often snap a small branch to swish around our head to keep the pesky mosquitos away. To this day, I rarely take a walk without keeping an eye out for a pretty stone to add to Mother's collection. Dorothy and I left the farm with an appreciation of nature's beauty surrounding us wherever we went.

Our Czech heritage remains important for its cultural significance, though not as much as for earlier generations who spoke the language, married fellow Czechs, and joined Sokol and Czech lodges. Dorothy visited Prague, and her son Geoffrey spent several years in the Czech Republic teaching English as a second language.

Art and I made several trips to Prague and travelled to rural towns where my ancestors had lived. Art taught fall semester of 2002 at the Economics University in Prague, which gave us a chance to live there as more than just tourists and do further traveling within the country. We rented an apartment for the semester, regularly took the subway, shopped in grocery stores, and enjoyed Czech beer and food in a variety of restaurants.

In 1994–95 we became friends with two Czech students, Petr Kohout and Jan Pesula, who were attending Colorado State University. Later, when Art and I went to Prague, we visited with Petr and Jan and their families. After Art passed away in 2020, I continued to be in touch with both of them. Petr last visited me in Parker, Colorado, in January 2024. He is an avid ice hockey fan and went to two Avalanche games while here! As a way to continue contact with Czech culture, I joined the Czechoslovak Genealogical Society International and attended their biannual convention in Milwaukee, Wisconsin, in October 2023.

Many Czech foods remained as part of our diet. Both Dorothy and I made *kolach*, but they never equaled our mother's. She made the closed kind, unlike the open-faced ones that are sold today. I have made *babovka*, a poppy seed cake which Mother made for holidays, as well as *houska*, the braided bread with poppy seed on top. Mother's pork roasts and sauerkraut continue to be a favorite of mine. She often made delicious plum dumplings which I never could master. Our Czech friend Petr introduced us to the herbal liqueur Becherovka, which Czechs down in a single swig, but I find

Janet by train station in Borova, where Joseph Makousky came from (left), Janet and Art traveling in the Czech Republic (right)

it to be more enjoyable sipped slowly. Czech foods definitely transferred down through the generations.

Dorothy and I were always interested in politics and international affairs, fostered by our parents who never failed to vote in an election. They took the daily *Minneapolis Tribune*, and regularly listened to news on the radio. Daddy, a Republican, and I, a Democrat, would argue politics but always respected that we each had a right to our opinion. While growing up, we never travelled outside the Minneapolis area, but we still had a wide view of the world and current events.

It was not surprising that once Dorothy and I graduated from high school, we went to college. Historically, the Czech culture emphasized intellectual achievements. Its history is filled with contributions to the arts, music, theatre, and literature. Dorothy and I didn't talk about college when growing up, but there was an underlying assumption that we would go. We had not come from an isolated rural area, but lived on the outskirts of Minneapolis where we were aware of the benefits of a college education. Many of our friends in school had already been accepted at universities when they graduated from high school. In the mid-1950s, increasing numbers of women attended college, often to become teachers or nurses. There was the joke then that women went to college to get their MRS degree! As a nation, we had not quite reached the point of accepting that a woman could aspire to have a professional career as well as being a wife and mother.

Dorothy and I knew that we would have to support ourselves through college, which meant we had to work and save money before attending. After high school, Dorothy enrolled in a seven-month secretarial course at the Minneapolis Business College and on April 30, 1956, began working for the Minneapolis law firm, Vennum, Newhall, Ackman, & Goetz. In the fall of 1957, she entered Hamline University, a logical choice as she had talked to Aunt Sylvia who graduated from Hamline.

Dorothy majored in political science with an interest in international relations, particularly the Middle East where she hoped to travel after graduation. During her junior year, she met Robert "Bob" Barrett, another political science major with similar interests. He was graduating from Hamline in the spring of 1960 and planned to go to American University for graduate work. After much pondering,

Dorothy agreed to get married in September 1960 and to finish her B.A. at American University, while Bob began work toward his Ph.D. In D.C., they both worked for Minnesota's 3rd congressional district's Congressman Clark MacGregor. After finishing their degrees, Dorothy and Bob returned to Minnesota. They made their home in Mankato, where Bob taught political science at Mankato State University and Dorothy taught at West High School for 30 years. Dorothy and Bob had two children, Geoffrey and Annie.

During Dorothy's teaching career, she went on to get a master's degree at the University of Minnesota. She took great interest in community issues and frequently wrote letters to the local newspaper on issues affecting health and safety. She did not shy away from controversies. Always active on the political front, she worked on several of the congressional campaigns of Tim Walz who represented the southern rural district, including Mankato.

Like Dorothy, I realized that I had to save money before I could go to college, so I worked at Minneapolis Honeywell Ordnance Division in Hopkins for two years as a secretary. My parents subsidized my education by my living at home, not paying rent, and using the family car. In return, I helped on the farm. I took my lunch to work from home and made the popular Tang drink from powder to save money. My father was not convinced that I should go to college and argued that in the end, I would make more money by working the four years instead of going to college. He did not resent my going to college but took a practical view of it, in part based on his struggle on the farm. My mother quietly supported my decision and assumed that I would follow Dorothy.

I entered Hamline University in the fall of 1960 and was very fearful that I would not succeed, mainly because I had been out of school for two years and all my classmates were fresh out of high school. The more vocal students intimidated me, so I virtually lived in the library stacks. But I surprised myself. In my sophomore year, I won a full tuition scholarship for being one of the top two women students. The top two women and top two men in each class received full tuition scholarships. To my amazement, I managed to keep this scholarship for the rest of my years at Hamline.

I became interested in travel programs, especially the Student Project for Amity Among Nations (SPAN) but lacked confidence that I could be accepted. I had a kindly political science professor and asked him if he thought I could do the program. He looked at me, smiled, and said, "Of course you can." I will always be grateful for his vote of confidence that led me to my first trip to Peru which sparked my interest in Latin America. In my junior year, I spent a semester at Drew University in New Jersey on a United Nations program. We went to the United Nations two days a week and took regular classes on campus the other days. This further increased my interest in international affairs.

At Hamline, I was a social studies major with a minor in education, with every intention to teach high school. But my student teaching experience was less than inspiring. I did a little teaching but had to record attendance and do other tedious chores with little student contact. I began to think of graduate school, just for an M.A.

I applied to several graduate schools. Fortunately, those were the days of the 1958 Title IV National Defense Education Act. This federal program was designed to alleviate a projected shortage of qualified college teachers. It created fellowships which guaranteed three years of graduate work toward the Ph.D. with an emphasis on language proficiency. The program provided tuition and expenses for the first year with the guarantee of a teaching assistantship for two years. I had offers from UCLA and Indiana University. I chose Indiana University where the faculty in Latin America history was stronger, especially with the recent hire of Professor James R. Scobie, whom I was grateful to have as my dissertation advisor.

Under the program at Indiana University, after I earned my M.A., I went right into the Ph.D. program with a history major and emphasis in Latin American Studies. In the summer of 1966, I returned to Peru to do a feasibility study on my dissertation topic, "Italians in Peru," which combined my interests in immigration and Latin America. In my last year at Indiana University, I met Art Worrall, who was finishing research for his dissertation. We married when I finished classes in the spring of 1967. That fall, we moved to Fort Collins where he had a position teaching Colonial American history at Colorado State University (CSU). In June 1969, he finished his dissertation for the Ph.D. In the fall semester of 1969, Art took a leave from CSU, and we went to Peru for my dissertation research. During the next few years, I wrote my dissertation and earned my Ph.D. in 1972. I subsequently got a teaching position at the University of Northern Colorado in Greeley, where I taught Latin American history, immigration history, and

American history. Art and I made our home in Fort Collins where we raised our three children: Tim, Beth, and Tom.

The educational journey that Dorothy and I took demonstrates generational changes. Our father left school after eighth grade, because as the oldest son his help was needed on the farm. Mother, living in the town of Hopkins and being able to work part time in her father's store, had the opportunity to attend and graduate from high school. Both our parents came from Czech immigrant backgrounds and lived in households where Czech was spoken. For them, further education was not an option, but they certainly had the ability. Being raised in the next generation, Dorothy and I had far greater opportunities, but we never lost sight of the work ethic and frugality we learned at home. We came from a stable, supportive family and a culture that valued education. We had cousins in college, and our neighbor Charley Neumeister, who worked his way through medical school, provided an example of what was possible. We were fortunate to be of this generation, and Dorothy and I took advantage of the opportunity to attend college and pursue careers.

Now in retirement, I am privileged to have the time to record the years from the early settlement in 1854 to the disappearance of the farm where my parents spent their lives, and where Dorothy and I grew up. Earlier generations did not have the luxury of time to leave a record.

Interstate 494, with its noise of rush hour traffic, has replaced the strawberry field and earlier pastureland where the cows grazed. No longer do the violets and mayflowers bloom that Dorothy and I

Janet and Dorothy (right) sitting on settee made by Steve Holasek which Dorothy had moved to her house in North Mankato, 2010.

picked on the way to visit our neighbors the Eckerts. Gone are the beautiful birch trees with their glistening white bark and whispering leaves. A water tower with "Eden Prairie" emblazoned on it rises above the night pasture where cows had grazed and looks down on where the raspberries once grew. The Lifetime Fitness Health Club now dominates the land where the house, barn, silo, corn crib, and iron picket fence once stood. No hint of the farm life that existed there 70 years earlier remains. Tennis balls bounce on the tennis courts which have replaced the flowers and vegetables that Mother planted by the pink house, a short distance away. It is the memory of this life and place which have now disappeared that this memoir strives to preserve for future generations.

Site of Holasek farm, 2022.

Evelyn by Holasek street sign.

Richard and Evelyn.

ACKNOWLEDGMENTS

The historian in me must first acknowledge the importance of Czech immigrant communities and their contributions to American culture. Most of the names of individuals and their stories, over several generations, have been lost to history. This memoir is an effort to recognize these unheard and forgotten voices.

I am indebted to many people who have contributed to this memoir. At Minnesota's Hopkins Historical Society, Mary Romportl gave me access to *The Hennepin County Review* and to the rich collection of materials, including photographs, pertaining to Czechs in Hopkins. Kathy Jorgenson helped me with online sources and has been my liaison in Colorado. The staffs of the St. Louis Park Historical Society and the Historical Society of Hennepin County provided me with detailed online information on the Glen Lake Farm School for Boys.

I have benefited from the friendship and help of a number of people. In the process of writing, Kenneth W. Rock suggested background readings on the Austrian Empire to give context to the Czech migration. Mary Alice and David G. McComb read the rough drafts and offered helpful comments. Fred and Virginia DeJohn Anderson gave me steady encouragement and advice in the use of tax documents. Jennifer Frost read the complete manuscript, making valuable suggestions. Daniel Tyler kindly put me in touch with the publisher of Spring Cedars, Audrey Zurcher. I was delighted with her interest in my memoir and her careful attention to detail as the process unfolded. I especially appreciated her willingness and encouragement to include family photos.

I am indebted to Alisa DiGiacomo, Senior Curator Emeritus, at History Colorado, for starting me on this journey several years ago by urging me to write a memoir. While working for her as a volunteer, I saw Alisa often. She followed my progress and never tired of my questions on content, organization, and style. Her comments on several drafts and our ongoing discussions on details have been invaluable.

I remain in contact with our Czech friends, Petr Kohout and Jan Pesula. Both gave freely of their time on several occasions when Art and I visited the Czech Republic. They took us on excursions to castles, museums, and restaurants where we spent hours discussing Czech culture, which gave me a greater understanding of my Czech heritage.

Jolene Kass has shared her extensive research with me on the Svec and Koblas families. Conversations with Jolene on Czechs in southern Minnesota, where she lives, helped me gain perspective on the area where many Czechs first settled. When I visited Mankato, Minnesota, in October 2022, Dorothy's friend Adeline Riha and I had numerous conversations on our common heritage. Adeline drove me around the Czech towns of Montgomery, Lonsdale, and New Prague where we dined on pork roast, dumplings, and a favorite Czech soup, *Vomachka*.

During this trip I spent a wonderful week in Hopkins with

my second cousin, Annette (Makousky) Greer. She drove me by the homes where Richard Holasek's parents and Stanley Svec's family had lived and to Glen Lake where the old Chastek house still stands. We went by the school that Dorothy and I attended in Eden Prairie. Over lunches and dinners we reminisced about our families and friends. I can never thank Annette enough for taking me to all the places I wanted to revisit from my childhood. On a cold, windy day, John LeBlanc, President and CEO of True Friends, kindly met us at the old Holasek house and opened it so we could wander through it and reminisce. Annette remembered the house from our childhood, when we played dolls together; her parents lived just a couple of miles away.

Family, of course, has been most important in telling this story. Over the years, my sister Dorothy and I had accumulated pictures, memorabilia, diaries, and assorted papers from our parents. These are the basis for much of this memoir. In numerous conversations, Dorothy's children Geoffrey and Annie shared their memories of their grandparents with me. In a fit of panic when I couldn't find the picture of the haystack that is on this cover, Annie discovered it in one of several boxes of photos left by her mother.

I am grateful to my late husband Art for his interest in my Czech heritage and spending a semester teaching at the University of Economics in Prague, which gave us a chance to live and travel in the Czech Republic as more than just tourists.

To my children Tim, Beth Newsom, and Tom, I owe the greatest debt for their encouragement, reading of drafts, and letting me reminisce with them, perhaps at too great a length. An extra thank you to Beth for her helpful revision of several chapters. In our many conversations, all three have helped me recall events that had slipped from my memory. They remember summer trips to visit Grandma and Grandpa in the pink house, Grandma's *kolach* and cookies, and especially barreling down the branch-strewn hill in the red wagon, laughing all the way. When my mother moved to Fort Collins, the grandchildren saw her more often. They had a chance to really get to know her and experience her kindness, sense of humor, and love. Finally, the next generation, my grandchildren Zoe, Madeleine, Lori, Luke, Matthew, William, and Emma helped in this process of writing by asking when it will be finished, looking at artifacts in the old trunk from Bohemia, and being amazed at how different things were when I grew up.

NOTES

CHAPTER 1

1. Hugh Agnew, *The Czechs and the Lands of the Bohemian Crown* (Stanford: Hoover Institution Press, 2004), 73–74. This book is an excellent source for a general history of the Czechs and the Bohemian Crownlands. For an example of the *robota,* see Thomas D. Hovel, "Robot Obligations of a Peasant Farmer in Bohemia," <u>Nase rodina,</u> *Quarterly of the Czechoslovak Genealogical Society International,* Vol. 35, No. 4, 164–167.

2. Wizard Marks, "Waves of Immigrants Settle Bohemian Flats and South Minneapolis," *The Alley,* May 1990, 9. Quoted from *The Bohemian Flats,* WPA Writers' Program, University of Minnesota Press: Minneapolis, 1941. *The Alley* is an independent, non-profit, monthly newspaper serving the Phillips neighborhood of Minneapolis.

3. Agnew, *The Czechs,* 89, 121.

4. Agnew, *The Czechs,* 88, 106.

5. Typescript by Clint Blomquist available at the Hopkins Historical Society. Blomquist (1903–1996) did more than anyone else to record the history of Hopkins, and many of his articles were carried in the *Hopkins Review.* He was one of the six founding members of the Hopkins Historical Society. He was helped by his wife, Viv, in assembling and storing acquisitions. He was in Evelyn Svec's high school graduation class in 1921.

6. Agnew, *The Czechs,* 85.

7. Jan Pesula provided this historical background in an email from Prague, May 27, 2022.

8. This account of arrival and the first few years is compiled from several sources: Jan M. Chastek's memoir published in *Amerikán Národní Kalendár,* Chicago, Illinois, reprinted in part in Beverly O. Ewing, ed., *Hopkins Minnesota Through the Years* (Hopkins: Hopkins Historical Society, 2002), 26–28; letter to Evelyn Holasek from her Aunt Carrie (Caroline Chastek Dominick) 1970. Also accounts by Vivian Allen, daughter of Evelyn's Uncle Frank Chastek, along with notes and pictures sent to this writer by Jan Streiff, daughter of Vivian Allen, Santa Rosa, California, September 3, 2011. For further information on Czech immigration, see articles by Esther Jerabek in *The Hennepin County Review* beginning on April 26, 1934, reprinted from her article in *Minnesota History* 1934.

CHAPTER 2

9 Much of this chapter comes from the recordings of Evelyn's memories, notes she kept on the Holasek family, and Jan M. Chastek's memoir.

CHAPTER 3

10 Glen Lake was never a town with specific boundaries, but a community of about one square mile at the crossroads of Excelsior Boulevard and Eden Prairie Road under the government of Minnetonka Township. At one time there had been an effort to incorporate it, but after an acrimonious discussion the decision was made to stay within the government of Minnetonka Township. The area's lake, known as Glen Lake, provided ice which the men cut for ice boxes before electric refrigerators. Ceil Robertson Marshall and Marion "Shorty" J. Stewart, *Glen Lake: A History of Glen Lake, Minnesota*, 1982, 5.

11 Early settlers squatted on government land. In the Pre-Emptive Act of 1841, Senator Henry Clay of Kentucky suggested a compromise to allow squatters to buy 160 acres of public land at the going price of $1.25/acre before it went up for public auction. This gave settlers the chance to buy land they occupied. Later, the Homestead Act of 1862 provided other means of gaining land.

12 Marshall and Stewart, *Glen Lake*, 5.

13 Letter to Evelyn Holasek from Aunt Carrie (Caroline Chastek Dominick) January 15, 1970.

14 Declaration for an Original Invalid Pension, January 11, 1890.

15 Testimony by Winslow Maly, age 54, resident of Los Angeles, CA, December 29, 1896.

16 "Hennepin County Home School Glen Lake School for Boys," *St. Louis Park Historical Society*; Annual Report, *Glen Lake Farm School for Boys*, Hennepin County Library, James K. Hosmer Special Collections Library; Betty Wilson, "Girls work out well at boys' home school," *The Minneapolis Star*, December 16, 1969, 33.

17 Mary Krugerud, *Interrupted Lives: The History of Tuberculosis in Minnesota and Glen Lake Sanatorium* (St. Cloud: North Star Press of St. Cloud, Inc., 2017), 22.

18 Krugerud, 227.

19 Letter to Evelyn Holasek from Aunt Carrie (Caroline Chastek Dominick), February 11, 1970.

20 "Pioneer Residents Fittingly Celebrate Golden Wedding," *Hennepin County Review*, March 19, 1918.

21 Vivian Chastek Allen, "From Childhood to our Marriage 1908–1929." Given to this writer by Vivian's daughter Jan Streiff.

22 Curt Brown, *Minnesota, 1918: When Flu, Fire and War Ravaged the State* (St. Paul: Minnesota Historical Society Press, 2018).

23 *Hennepin County Review*, September 14, 1933.

CHAPTER 4

24 Jolene Kass, great granddaughter of Evelyn's Aunt Rose Pauline Svec Koblas, has done extensive genealogy research on the Svec and Koblas families which is posted on Ancestry.com. She furnished much of the information on the Koblas family in this chapter.

25 *Hennepin County Enterprise,* August, 1919.

26 Eventually John and Rose Pauline settled in Lesterville, South Dakota where John and his brother Frank started a Meat Market. They lived there for seven years before returning to Minnesota—Ogema and then Hopkins—where John died of alcoholism in 1918. Their family of six children, Alice Rose, Mabel, John, Rose Agnes, Blanche, and George, all lived in the Minneapolis area and Rose Pauline went to live with them after her husband's death. She was living with her son John when she died in 1942. Michael Koblas (1864–1933) settled in Hopkins and worked as a shoemaker. Frank (1872–1946) was the only Koblas member to stay in South Dakota where he died in Lesterville in 1946.

27 Bill Beyer, "Jumping the tracks, paying the freight," *Hennepin History* 81, No. 3, 2022.

28 Roman L. Hruska, "A Brief History of 'Western Bohemian,'" published in the Fiftieth Anniversary Convention Program (1947, Omaha, Nebraska). This document detailing the history of Czechoslovak benevolent societies is on file at the Hopkins Historical Society. Member dues provided insurance protection for burial expenses. The fraternal society also provided social activities and a way for new immigrants to meet and "relieve their sharp loneliness." "Landmark of Glen Lake Destroyed by Fire Early Sunday," *Hennepin County Review,* January 5, 1933, 1.

29 *Hennepin County Enterprise,* July 2, 1925.

30 The curative value of manure is questionable, but at that time it was credited as saving Sylvia's life.

CHAPTER 5

[31] Chad Sewich, "Using History to Determine the Strength of the 1925 Hopkins Tornado," *Hopkins News,* No. 2, 2022, 1–3.

[32] *The Hennepin County Review*, June 4, 1925.

[33] Summarized from *The Hennepin County Review,* May 10, 17, 31, June 7, 28, 1934.

[34] *The Hennepin County Review,* June 14, 1934.

[35] *Hopkins Historical Society,* No. 2, 2021. This issue is devoted to raspberry growing.

CHAPTER 6

[36] Evelyn Holasek's Diaries, 1931, 1932.

[37] In early 1935 Northern States Power put in electric lines. This was before Congress created the Rural Electrification Administration in 1935 which brought electric power to farmers through utility cooperatives.

CHAPTER 7

[38] Jensen, a laborer, is listed as living with Richard and Evelyn as a lodger in the 1940 Federal Census.

CHAPTER 14

[39] David M. Oshinsky, *Polio An American Story* (New York: Oxford University Press, 2006) Chapter 12.

ABOUT THE AUTHOR

Janet E. Holasek Worrall grew up on a farm in Eden Prairie, Minnesota, then a rural area southwest of the Twin Cities. She received her B.A. from Hamline University and her M.A. and Ph.D. from Indiana University where she specialized in Latin American history. She was a professor of history at the University of Northern Colorado, teaching for over 30 years. Her research and publications focused on Latin America, Immigration, Italian and German Prisoners of War, and Italian immigration in the Denver area.

Janet lived in Fort Collins, Colorado, with her husband Arthur and their three children. In 2015, she and Arthur moved to Parker, Colorado, to be closer to their children and grandchildren. Janet presently volunteers at History Colorado and enjoys working on its Italian American Preservation collection. In her spare time, she participates in two book clubs, a choir, and continues her lifetime hobby of gardening, growing tomatoes, cucumbers, peppers and more, and tending her twenty African violets.

www.ingramcontent.com/pod-product-compliance
Lightning Source LLC
Chambersburg PA
CBHW050552170426
43201CB00011B/1672